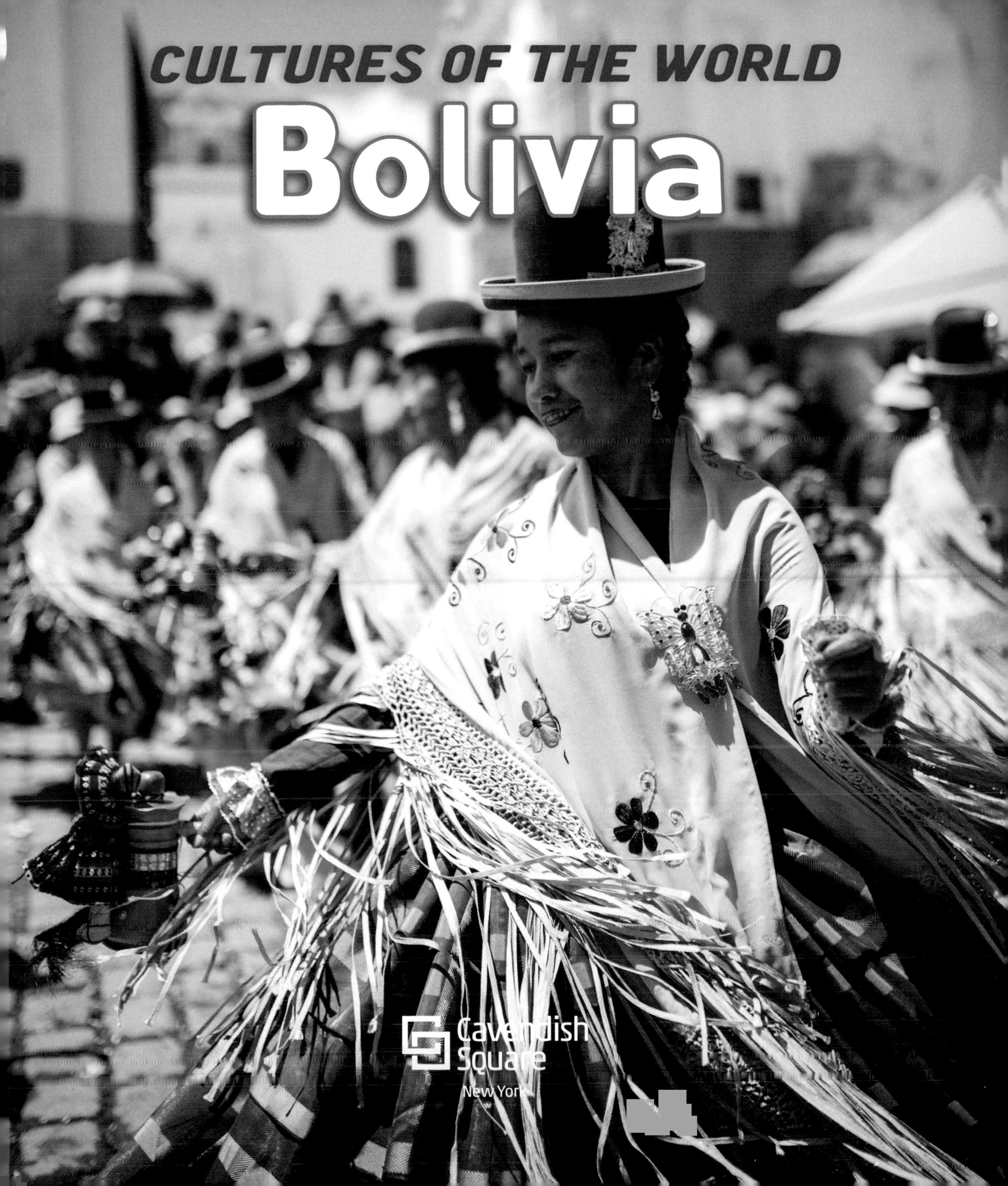
CULTURES OF THE WORLD
Bolivia
Cavendish
Square
New York

Published in 2017 by Cavendish Square Publishing, LLC
243 5th Avenue, Suite 136, New York, NY 10016

Third Edition

CPSIA Compliance Information: Batch #CS16CSQ
All websites were available and accurate when this book was sent to press.

Library of Congress Cataloging-in-Publication Data

Names: Pateman, Robert, 1954- author. | Cramer, Marcus, author. | Nevins, Debbie, author.
Title: Bolivia / Robert Pateman, Marcus Cramer and Debbie Nevins.
Description: New York: Cavendish Square Pub., 2017. | Series: Cultures of the world | Includes bibliographical references and index.
Identifiers: LCCN 2016003472 (print) | LCCN 2016004053 (ebook) | ISBN 9781502618382 (library bound) | ISBN 9781502618399 (ebook)
Classification: LCC F3308.5 .P37 2017 (print) | LCC F3308.5 (ebook) | DDC 984--dc23
LC record available at http://lccn.loc.gov/2016003472

Writers: Robert Pateman, Marcus Cramer; Debbie Nevins, third edition
Editorial Director, third edition: David McNamara
Editor, third edition: Debbie Nevins
Art Director, third edition: Jeffrey Talbot
Designer, third edition: Jessica Nevins
Production Assistant, third edition: Karol Szymczuk
Cover Picture Researcher: Jeffrey Talbot
Picture Researcher, third edition: Jessica Nevins

PICTURE CREDITS

The photographs in this book are used with the permission of: Will Steeley/Alamy, cover; Ben Pipe/robertharding, 1; Vladimir Krupenkin/Shutterstock.com, 3; © Santiago Urquijo/Moment/Getty Images, 5; Jose Luis Quintana/LatinContent/Getty Images, 6; José Luis Quintana/LatinContent/Getty Images, 7; AP Photo/Joao Padua, 8; Shanti Hesse/Shutterstock.com, 9; wuthrich didier/Shutterstock.com, 10; saiko3p/Shutterstock.com, 11; Shanti Hesse/Shutterstock.com, 13; Elzbieta Sekowska/Shutterstock.com, 14; Helen Filatova/Shutterstock.com, 15; Serjio74/Shutterstock.com, 16; Matyas Rehak/Shutterstock.com, 17; Elzbieta Sekowska/Shutterstock.com, 18; Stefano Buttafoco/Shutterstock.com, 20; Michel Piccaya/Shutterstock.com, 22; Stefano Buttafoco/Shutterstock.com, 23; Charles Phelps Cushing/ClassicStock/Getty Images, 24; Elisa Locci/Shutterstock.com, 25; JORGE BERNAL/AFP/Getty Images, 26; Antonio Salguero/DEA PICTURE LIBRARY/De Agostini Picture, 28; AP-Photo/El Diario, 31; Keystone-France/Gamma-Keystone via Getty Images, 32; GONZALO ESPINOZA/AFP/Getty Images, 33; Frederic Legrand - COMEO/Shutterstock.com, 34; jjspring/Shutterstock.com, 36; stocklight/Shutterstock.com, 39; Javier Mamani/LatinContent/Getty Images, 41; Klaus Balzano/Shutterstock.com, 42; T photography/Shutterstock.com, 44; Aizar Raldes Nunez/AFP/Getty Images, 46; Free Wind 2014/Shutterstock.com, 48; T photography/Shutterstock.com, 50; africa924/Shutterstock.com, 52; hecke61/Shutterstock.com, 54; Klaus Balzano/Shutterstock.com, 56; Jami Tarris/Photographer's Choice/Getty Images, 58; AP Photo/Juan Karita, 61; Ruslana Iurchenko/Shutterstock.com, 62; Aizar Raldes Nunez/AFP/Getty Images, 65; Ben Speck & Karin Ananiassen/Getty Images, 66; Jose Luis Quintana/LatinContent/Getty Images, 70; Inga Locmele/Shutterstock.com, 72; nouseforname /Shutterstock.com, 74; PavelSvoboda/Shutterstock.com, 75; flocu/Shutterstock.com, 76; nouseforname/Shutterstock.com, 77; Michel Piccaya /Shutterstock.com, 78; AIZAR RALDES/AFP/GettyImages, 79; Melanie Stetson Freeman/The Christian Science Monitor via Getty Images, 80; STR/AFP/Getty Images, 82; Byelikova Oksana/Shutterstock.com, 83; Byelikova Oksana/Shutterstock.com, 84; Stefano Buttafoco/Shutterstock.com, 86; Amanecer Tedesqui/LatinContent/Getty Images, 90; © James Brunker/Alamy Stock Photo, 92; CRIS BOURONCLE/AFP/Getty Images, 94; RODRIGO BUENDIA/AFP/Getty Images, 95; Michel Piccaya/Shutterstock.com, 97; Pyty/Shutterstock.com, 98; Ruslana Iurchenko/Shutterstock.com, 100; Vlad Karavaev/Shutterstock.com, 101; Tyler Bridges/Miami Herald/MCT via Getty Images, 103; Ruslana Iurchenko/Shutterstock.com, 104; Andrey Gontarev/Shutterstock.com, 104; GUSTAVO SEGOVIA,GUSTAVO SEGOVIA/AFP/Getty Images, 106; Insights/UIG via Getty Images, 107; AIZAR RALDES/AFP/Getty Images, 109; Popperfoto/Getty Images, 110; mezzotint/Shutterstock.com, 112; AP Photo, 113; Jess Kraft/Shutterstock.com, 114; AIZAR RALDES/AFP/Getty Images, 116; Andrey Gontarev/Shutterstock.com, 117; Byelikova Oksana/Shutterstock.com, 118; AIZAR RALDES/AFP/Getty Images, 119; ChiccoDodiFC/Shutterstock.com, 120; Nathalie Stroobant/Shutterstock.com, 122; Klaus Ulrich Mueller/Shutterstock.com, 124; Fabio Lamanna/Shutterstock.com, 125; Ildi Papp/Shutterstock.com, 126; Ildi Papp/Shutterstock.com, 127; Ildi Papp/Shutterstock.com, 128; Ildi Papp/Shutterstock.com, 129; Tyler Nevins, 130; Tyler Nevins, 131.

PRECEDING PAGE

Dancers in traditional dress perform at the Fiesta de la Virgen de la Candelaria in Copacabana, Bolivia

Printed in the United States of America

CONTENTS

BOLIVIA TODAY 5

1. GEOGRAPHY
The different regions • Mountains • Rivers, swamps, and lakes • Climate • Flora and fauna • The disputed capitals 11

2. HISTORY
The Incas • Arrival of the Spanish • Spain declines • The fight for freedom • Losing ground • The Chaco War • Revolution and reform • Instability • Indigenous people power 21

3. GOVERNMENT
The constitution • The executive • The legislature • The judiciary • The electoral process and political parties • Local government and autonomy • Foreign policy 37

4. ECONOMY
Natural resources • Agriculture • Industry • Child labor 45

5. ENVIRONMENT
Protected areas • Threatened species • Deforestation • Water pollution • Climate change 55

6. BOLIVIANS
The indigenous highlanders • The indigenous lowlanders • The Spanish • The mestizos • The Afro-Bolivians • New arrivals 63

7. LIFESTYLE
Urban poor • Health care • Padrinos • Childhood and growing up • Education • Weddings • Role of women • Traditional dress 73

8. RELIGION
The Incan religion • The old gods survive • Influence of the Jesuits • Miracles and pilgrimages • Liberation theology • Cha'lla • Witchcraft and wisdom **85**

9. LANGUAGE
Quechua and Aymara • Spanish **93**

10. ARTS
Dance • Visual arts • Traditional music **99**

11. LEISURE
Children's games • Traditional sports • A nation of soccer lovers • Other sports • Weekends **107**

12. FESTIVALS
New Year's • Alasitas Festival • Oruro Festival • Easter • Fiesta del Gran Poder • Inti Raymi / Fiesta de San Juan Batista • Fiesta del Espíritu • Christmas • Historic and political holidays **115**

13. FOOD
Potatoes and other tubers • The meal pattern • Favorite recipes • Fruits and desserts • Street food • Drinks **123**

MAP OF BOLIVIA **133**

ABOUT THE ECONOMY **135**

ABOUT THE CULTURE **137**

TIMELINE **138**

GLOSSARY **140**

FOR FURTHER INFORMATION **141**

BIBLIOGRAPHY **142**

INDEX **143**

BOLIVIA TODAY

IN MANY WAYS, BOLIVIA IS A VERY RICH COUNTRY. IT HAS A wealth of natural resources, vast biodiversity, beautiful landscapes, and fascinating cultures. The country has snowcapped mountain ranges, deep gorges, fertile valleys, and a steamy jungle region that serves as the gateway to the Amazon. Enormous mineral wealth lies inside those mountains, and a huge reserve of lithium lies beneath the world's largest salt flat in southwest Bolivia. Ancient Incan civilization and the Spanish colonial rule have combined to produce a distinctive cultural heritage. Ancestral gods persist within the rituals of modern Roman Catholicism. Spanish festivals incorporate Incan customs. A tradition of lively dance, haunting music, and colorful weaving keeps old traditions alive. The people themselves represent a global variety of ethnic backgrounds, all contributing to the multicultural mix. Such a country should be a top tourist attraction. Indeed, in 2010, more than eighty thousand people visited Bolivia's magnificent mountains, lush rainforests, and historic cities.

With all that, Bolivia is the poorest nation in South America. The reasons for this surprising fact are many, and are detailed in this book. Thieves of the country's

wealth have included the usual suspects—wars, violence, greed, culture clashes, inequality, exploitation, oppression, political instability—the list of historical evils that Bolivia has experienced is long and sad.

In a conflict more than a century ago, the country lost its coastal land on the Pacific Ocean to Chile, and became landlocked. Bolivia has been trying to win back that connection to the sea ever since. Until then, it is closed off from one of the most important natural resources of all. The loss of sea access affects Bolivia at more than just an economic level. A play called *Mar* (*Sea*), performed in 2015 by the country's Teatro Los Andes in La Paz, focused on the nation's longing for the sea. Said Alice Guimareaes, one of the actors, "In the play ... we try to reflect on what it means to have lost the sea. What is this sea, why do we want to get it back, what is our sea?"

Bolivians demonstrate for access to the sea in September 2015 after the International Court of Justice agreed to hear Bolivia's maritime claim against Chile.

In the last decade or so, Bolivia has gone through some important changes. After decades of bad leadership—from strong-armed dictators to merely ineffective or unethical presidents—Bolivians made history in 2005 by electing the first indigenous person to lead the country. Evo Morales is ethnically Aymara, a former coca farmer, labor union leader, and socialist who was active in the anti-government revolts that precipitated the country's strong swing to the left. He quickly set out to reverse centuries of what he sees as the oppressive and unfair policies that have piped most of Bolivia's wealth into the pockets of the Spanish-descended elite and, even more, out of the country altogether.

Morales directed the writing of a new constitution, nationalized the natural gas industry, gave equal status and increased autonomy to

President Evo Morales (in green) plays a celebratory soccer game at the opening of a gas processing plant in 2013.

the indigenous peoples, and even gave the country a new name—the Plurinational State of Bolivia. He aligned himself with fellow leftist leaders in Latin America, and kicked out the US ambassador and agents, the US Drug Enforcement Administration, and the US Agency for International Development (USAID). Naturally, these actions did not sit well with the United States, but they made Morales extremely popular with his people. In 2014, the fifty-four-year-old president was signed to the roster of Sport Boys, a professional football (soccer) team in Santa Cruz. He signed for the minimum salary of about $214. Morales is a huge soccer fan and somehow has time to play with the pros.

Although he changed the country's official status to that of a secular rather than Roman Catholic nation, which it had been from the times of the Spanish Conquest, Morales heartily welcomed Pope Francis on the papal tour of South America in October 2015.

From 2005 to 2014, Bolivia's economy grew impressively, and extreme poverty rates went down; but deeply entrenched poverty cannot be eradicated in just a few years. Despite this growth, Bolivia today remains the poorest country in South America because it has such a long way to go. The good news is that the country has tremendous potential, if its internal problems don't cause this upward trajectory to collapse. Morales is now in his third term, a constitutional prohibition that he maneuvered around on technicalities, but he and his supporters are reportedly interested in having him seek a fourth term. Much will depend on whether the economy's growth and the president's popularity continue.

Morales is certainly not without his detractors, as protest signs in Bolivia declaring "No Re-Re-Re-Relection" make clear. He has tended to make provocative statements, such as his comment in 2013 that he was "almost certain" that "the empire" [the United States] had poisoned his political ally, the late Venezuelan president Hugo Chavez, who died of cancer that year. Morales has also accused the United States of actively working to undermine him, and even, perhaps, to kill him.

Residents of Santa Cruz hold signs saying "Evo, killer, resign" during an anti-government protest in 2007.

"They [US officials] accuse me of everything," Morales said at a campaign rally in 2008. "They say Evo is a drug trafficker, that Evo is a narcoterrorist." Indeed, there are some critics internationally who charge exactly that. The issue is coca, the plant from which cocaine is derived. Coca—not cocaine, but the natural coca leaf—is extremely important to the indigenous people who chew the leaves as a mild stimulant. In fact, Bolivia's new constitution protects the legal status of coca, but bans cocaine.

Packaged coca leaves are ready for sale in La Paz.

Nevertheless, it's an open secret that Bolivia has a shadow (illegal) economy based on coca farming for the production of cocaine. It is said to be the country's true top export. It might seem odd that a former coca farmer would work to limit production of coca, but Morales is doing just that. According to the UN Office on Drugs and Crime, Bolivia's coca production fell by 34 percent from 2010 to 2014. Bolivia is reportedly very close to meeting its goal of limiting the cultivation of coca for traditional and other legal uses to only 20,000 hectares (about 49,500 acres).

For Bolivia, the gargantuan task of improving its legal economy and eradicating extreme poverty won't be easy, especially while simultaneously reducing its role in the illegal drug trade. For everyday Bolivians, these years of rapid change are both a challenge and a time of optimism. Although Bolivia's ancient traditions and ways of life struggle to survive in this uncertain and sometimes hostile global environment, its people remain hopeful of a better future.

GEOGRAPHY

Cactuses grow in the desert surrounding the Salar de Uyuni salt flats in southwestern Bolivia.

1

Altitude has more influence on the climate of Bolivia than the seasons do. A visitor can experience a change in climate just by walking up or down a thousand feet or so on a Bolivian footpath.

BOLIVIA IS THE HIGHEST AND MOST isolated country in South America. With no direct access to the sea, it's one of only two landlocked countries on the continent—the other is Paraguay—and it is South America's poorest nation.

Covering 424,164 square miles (1,098,580 square kilometers), Bolivia is a large country that's twice the size of Texas. However, it is dwarfed by its much bigger neighbors Brazil and Argentina.

The red roofs of Sucre are seen from the vantage point of La Recoleta Monastery.

Despite its name, which means "swampy plain," Cochabamba is one of Bolivia's most pleasant cities, with a climate similar to Mediterranean Europe. It is surrounded by rich farmland, which has earned the region the title of "breadbasket of Bolivia."

Bolivia shares borders with Peru and Chile to the west, Argentina to the south, Paraguay to the southeast, and Brazil to the east and north. Most of the population lives on the High Plateau, or Altiplano (ahl-tee-PLAH-noh), between two chains of the Andes Mountains. Most people would consider this region to be "typically Bolivian." However, the country also has large areas of tropical rain forest, savanna, swamp, and semidesert.

Ironically, for such a poor country, Bolivia has rich resources of oil and minerals, but they have been largely exploited by foreign corporations and the wealth taken out of the country. Bolivia's considerable natural gas resources, also mostly foreign-owned, were nationalized in recent years by President Evo Morales, thus returning them to Bolivian control.

THE DIFFERENT REGIONS

Bolivia has three main regions: the Altiplano or High Plateau, the valleys, and the lowlands. The Altiplano is one of the highest inhabited areas in the world. This plateau lies between two ranges of the Andes Mountains at an average height of 12,000 feet (3,600 meters). It is a high, bleak, windswept, cold, and barren region. Parts of the Altiplano are vast areas of solitude, while other parts, especially around the city of La Paz, are more densely populated than any other region of Bolivia.

The valleys include the Yungas, which are deep valleys and high ridges on the eastern slopes of the Andes, and cities such as Cochabamba, Sucre, and Tarija are located in the wider valleys. The Yungas are noted for their rugged terrain; hills and gorges tangle into each other, making many areas almost inaccessible. Although some valleys are narrow, others fan out into well-watered, fertile basins. This land is more fertile and more hospitable than the Altiplano, with a milder climate. Thirty percent of the population of Bolivia lives in the valleys, which contain 40 percent of the country's cultivated land.

The lowlands, which lie to the north and east and stretch to Brazil and Paraguay, make up about two-thirds of Bolivia. The area around Trinidad is covered with rich tropical forests, part of the Amazon River basin. Other areas are open savannas or swamps. In the south the lowlands become the South Bolivian Chaco, part of the Gran Chaco. For seven to eight months,

THE LEGEND OF ILLIMANI

Bolivian indigenous culture has many wonderful legends. According to the legend of Mount Illimani, two mountains once stood above the place where the city of La Paz now stands. The god who created them could never decide which he loved the most. Both looked different in different light, and he was always walking across the canyon floor to see them at their best.

*The god was watching Mount Illimani one day when he decided it really was his favorite. Using his sling, he hurled a giant boulder at the other peak, and the mountaintop rolled far away. The god cried, "*Sajama!*" which means "Go away!" The mountain, where it came to rest, is still called by that name. The lower half of the mountain in its original place is called* Mururata, *which means "beheaded."*

this is a semidesert, but it turns into a swamp when the rains arrive. This is one of the hottest parts of South America during the rainy season, when temperatures of 100 degrees Fahrenheit (37.8 degrees Celsius) are common. The Chaco is sparsely populated, as are the lowlands generally.

MOUNTAINS

The Andes Mountains run the entire length of South America, from the northern coast of the Caribbean Sea to Tierra del Fuego at the southern end of Chile, a distance of 5,500 miles (8,850 km). Before they enter Bolivia, the Andes divide into two ranges. The Cordillera Occidental runs through the west of the country and forms Bolivia's border with Chile. There are several active volcanoes in this range, and they occasionally give off gases. The highest point is Mount Sajama at 21,463 feet (6,542 m).

The La Paz fire brigade is seldom called on to put out fires because it is so difficult for flames to spread with the low oxygen density found at such high altitude. However, during the rainy season, floods keep the fire brigade very busy.

The Cordillera Oriental passes to the east and reaches its most impressive section, called Cordillera Real, around La Paz, where there is a towering line of snowcapped peaks. The most famous of these is Mount Illimani at 21,200 feet (6,462 m). This extraordinary mountain range has more than six hundred peaks that are higher than 16,400 feet (5,000 m).

Farther south the Andes come back together into one range and widen. This forms the area known as the Puna. The Andes are rich in mineral deposits, including zinc, tin, and silver.

RIVERS, SWAMPS, AND LAKES

Bolivia has three drainage systems: the Amazon system in the northwest, north, and northeast; the Lake Titicaca system in the Altiplano; and a third that carries water southwest toward Argentina.

The Beni and Mamoré Rivers collect much of the water that flows east from the Andes and form headwaters of the Amazon River. Many rivers on the plains are deep enough to take shallow draft boats and barges and are important for transportation in an area where there are few roads. It is not possible to travel along the rivers to the Amazon proper and the sea beyond because of rapids.

Local people travel in a traditional wooden boat on the Beni River.

A second drainage system starts on the Altiplano with hundreds of streams flowing down from the snow line into Lake Titicaca. The Desaguadero River flows south from Titicaca into Lake Poopó, a shallow, salty body of water rarely more than 10 feet (3 m) deep. It usually covers 1,000 square miles (2,500 sq km), but after a heavy rain the lake can expand to the edge of Oruro, 30 miles (45 km) away.

The Lacajahuira River flows south from Poopó and empties into the Coipasa Salt Field. This is a wide, marshy, salt-encrusted wilderness with one small body of water at its lowest point. The magnificently desolate Uyuni Salt Flat lies farther south and is even bigger, covering 4,085 square miles (10,580 sq km).

The third drainage system is made up of water that runs off the Yungas and flows south into the Pilcomayo River and its tributaries. These run southeast to join the Paraguay and the Plate Rivers.

Salar de Uyuni, in southwest Bolivia, is the world's largest salt flat, the remains of a prehistoric lake that went dry.

CLIMATE

Because Bolivia is situated in the Southern Hemisphere, its summer and winter are the reverse of the seasons in the Northern Hemisphere. Summer brings the most rain. Winter is generally drier and more pleasant, with day after day of clear blue skies. The higher areas get cold, and between June and August the fierce *surazo* (soo-RAH-zoh) winds blow in from the Argentine pampas, bringing storms and severe drops in temperature to the normally hot eastern lowlands.

The eastern slopes of the Andes mountain ranges below 6,000 feet (1,829 m) have a tropical climate. Average rainfall is 30 to 50 inches (76—127 cm) and neither temperature nor rainfall varies much. The Yungas, 6,000 to 9,500 feet (1,829—2,896 m), are seldom cold. This area has the most pleasant climate, often described as permanent spring. The Altiplano zone is always cool. Summer brings thunderstorms and winter brings occasional snow. Above 13,000 feet (3,962 m), there are arctic conditions.

Residents greet visitors on one of the floating islands of Lake Titicaca.

FLORA AND FAUNA

Bolivia's vegetation is as varied as its climate. On the Altiplano only hardy plants survive. *Ichu*, a coarse bunched grass, is the most common vegetation and is the basic food of the llama. *Thola*, a wind-resistant shrub, also grows here, as do cacti. Along the banks of Lake Titicaca *totora* reeds are abundant. Native *quishuara* and *khena* trees grow on the Altiplano, and eucalyptus and pine trees have been introduced around the lake.

The Yungas have a wide range of natural trees, including cedar, mahogany, and walnut. One of the most useful is the *cinchona*, from which the malaria-fighting drug quinine was first extracted.

In the lowland plains the Bolivian rain forest contains hundreds of species of trees, many of which grow to enormous heights. An equally diverse range of plants grows under the forest canopy.

The northern and central lowlands consist of grassy savannas and isolated woodlands, but farther south in the Chaco, little survives the fierce conditions except cacti and scorched grasses.

LAKE TITICACA

Lake Titicaca is remarkable because of its size, its altitude, and its great beauty. It is the second-largest lake in South America, covering 3,200 square miles (8,288 sq km), and has forty-one islands. It's impossible to see the northwestern shore from the lakeside town of Copacabana. Its beauty comes from a combination of its deep color, the reflection of the blue sky, and in the south, the backdrop of mountain peaks.

In fact, Titicaca is almost two lakes; the smaller southern body of water is joined to the main lake only by a narrow strait. The border between Peru and Bolivia goes through the center of the lake, which means that traffic from La Paz has to cross the strait by ferry, rather than take the western shoreline route that would cross the Peruvian border. Buses and cars go across on small platform rafts, like the one pictured above, while passengers transfer to little speedboats.

Titicaca lies at an altitude of 12,500 feet (3,810 m) and is the highest navigable body of water in the world. It is also an exceptionally deep lake, reaching depths of about 900 feet (274 m).

The lake played an important role in the religious beliefs of the early civilizations of the area. The Incas believed this was the spot where humankind was created. Rumors still persist that Lake Titicaca holds great hidden treasures. According to some accounts, the Incas threw vast amounts of gold and silver into the lake to prevent it from being stolen by the Spanish. Other legends tell of ancient cities hidden beneath the deep waters.

Capybaras are semiaquatic rodents that grow to be about 3 to 4 feet (90–122 cm) long.

Bolivia's wildlife is equally varied. The llama, alpaca, guanaco, and vicuña, all native to the Andes, live in the highlands. The llama and alpaca are domesticated versions of the guanaco. The vicuña is not kept domestically, but it is heavily hunted for its silky wool.

The Altiplano is also home to several species of rodents, including the cavy, a guinea pig bred for its meat and often kept as a pet.

Lake Titicaca is home to many different species of birds, including gulls, ducks, geese, and hummingbirds. Lake Poopó to the south is famous for its once endangered flamingos.

The swamps and plains of the lowlands have a very different ecosystem. Here are anteaters; wild pigs called peccaries; pumas; marsh deer; and the capybara, the world's largest rodent. The rivers and swamps also support countless numbers of fish, frogs, butterflies, toads, and lizards. The most remarkable bird of the region is the rhea, a large, flightless bird similar to an ostrich.

Many of these animals are hunted for food. The armadillo is considered a delicacy, and its shell can be used to make musical instruments. The reason wildlife has survived so well is that the region has remained sparsely populated until recently.

The most diverse wildlife of all is concentrated in Bolivia's tropical forests. Mammals include monkeys, anteaters, tapirs, jaguars, and the spectacled bear. The rivers are alive with fish, including the meat-eating piranha, and there are hundreds of species of birds and thousands of species of insects.

Bolivia's environment is facing new problems as roads are constructed to open up previously inaccessible areas, threatening Bolivia's wildlife.

THE DISPUTED CAPITALS

Sucre was the capital at Bolivia's independence and is still the constitutional capital, but legislative and executive functions are located in La Paz. La Paz is the second largest city in Bolivia, with a population rising toward the one million mark. About half of the population is of native birth. La Paz was founded in 1548 by Alonso de Mendoza. The Spaniards hoped to find gold here but were disappointed. Instead, La Paz survived because of its position on the trade route between Potosí and Lima, Peru. It is the political and commercial center of the nation.

Sucre lies southeast of La Paz. It has not grown as large as La Paz, but most people from Sucre believe their city is more beautiful, and it certainly has a milder, more pleasant climate. Founded in 1539, Sucre is still the most Spanish-looking of Bolivia's cities, with many old colonial buildings with white facades and orange tile roofs.

Recently Santa Cruz has become the largest city in Bolivia, as well as the industrial center of the country. Santa Cruz has considerable economic influence and is currently competing with La Paz in the realm of political dominance.

The Incas had a special respect for the puma. According to Bolivian folklore, when some of the moon disappears, it means that the puma has crept up and taken a bite out of it.

INTERNET LINKS

ngm.nationalgeographic.com/2008/07/bolivias-new-order/altiplano-guillermoprieto-text
This *National Geographic* feature includes a section on the Altiplano, with an interactive photo map.

www.peakware.com/areas.html?a=316
This mountaineering site has maps and photos of each of Bolivia's major peaks.

www.sacred-destinations.com/bolivia/lake-titicaca
This overview of Lake Titicaca focuses on its significance in Incan myth.

www.worldatlas.com/webimage/countrys/samerica/bolivia/boland.htm#page
This site has a basic overview of Bolivia's geography and other features.

HISTORY

The entrance to the Kalasasaya Temple frames the Ponce Monolith at the Tiwanaku ruins in Bolivia.

2

Between 1825 and 1982, Bolivia is said to have experienced nearly two hundred coups d'etat.

THE FIRST HUMANS TO INHABIT THE region that would become Bolivia were probably nomadic hunters. Like all native people on the American continents, they were descendents of people who crossed the Bering Strait from Siberia and, over the centuries, moved southward through the Americas.

By 1500 BCE, human civilization was well established on the Altiplano, the high plateau between the two parallel mountain ranges that run north-south in western Bolivia. Tiwanaku, a pre-Columbian archaeological site on Lake Titicaca, was then a small agricultural village. The lifestyle of the hunter-gatherers eventually changed as they developed agriculture. Between 800 BCE and 500 BCE, the people began cultivating the potato and had herds of domesticated llamas and alpacas. Over time, Tiwanaku grew into the political and religious center of a powerful empire. The ruins at the site show that these people had developed the technology to convey enormous blocks of building stone across Lake Titicaca.

At its height, Tiwanaku had a population of around twenty thousand people, but after three hundred or four hundred years it fell into decline. Nobody is sure why this happened. It might have been due to war, or perhaps to one of the extended drought periods that has affected the area in cyclical climate changes. Tiwanaku was abandoned around 1000 CE.

Ancient Incan ruins called the Palace of the Sun remain on Isla del Sol (Island of the Sun) in Lake Titicaca.

THE INCAS

The decline of the Tiwanaku Empire left a power vacuum that was eventually filled by the dramatic rise of the Incan Empire.

The Incas originally came from the Cuzco Valley in Peru, but from around 1400 CE they expanded to build an empire that stretched for 2,000 miles (3,220 km) and probably had, according to various specialists' estimates, between five million and twelve million subjects. To gain more control over the resistant native Aymara people, the Incas moved many speakers of their own language into the region.

The Incas were magnificent organizers and engineers. They constructed great cities linked by stone roads and established a system of runners to carry messages between cities. They built suspension bridges across wide gorges and terraced the mountainsides to grow crops.

Incan artists worked in ceramics, silver, and gold. Their weavers produced magnificent textiles. These were so fine that the Spanish mistook Incan cotton for silk. Incan culture was rich in music and dance and had wonderful legends and folktales that were passed on by word of mouth. Many are still told today.

The Incas neither used the wheel nor developed a system of writing. The Incan Empire left two major legacies: the ruins of their great cities and a language, Quechua, which continues to be spoken throughout much of South America. The Incan Empire lasted about a hundred years before the Spanish conquered it. Whether Incan culture was already in decline by then is debatable, but the Incas were certainly no match for the better-armed invaders who reached the borders of their empire in 1532.

ARRIVAL OF THE SPANISH

In 1492, Christopher Columbus became the first European since the Vikings to sail to the American continents. Pope Alexander VI decreed that this

TIWANAKU

The archaeological site of Tiwanaku (also spelled Tiahuanaco) lies less than two hours' drive from La Paz. It is not, at first glance, a particularly impressive site because much of the stone has been carried away over the years to build churches and bridges.

There remain the mound of the Akapana, a great step pyramid, and the Kalasasaya, a great sunken temple. Just visible through the archway is the large sculpted figure that stands outside the Kalasasaya. Other sculptures include several freestanding statues, two carved doorways, and some stone faces in the walls of the sunken temple.

For archaeologists Tiwanaku is an interesting site that continues to produce surprises. Excavations in this century have revealed that the site was not just an isolated ceremonial center, as first thought, but a bustling metropolis that was home to thousands of people.

Scientists have discovered evidence of a system of raised fields, which both protected the crops from the waters of Lake Titicaca and retained heat during the cold Altiplano nights. The center of the pyramid has yet to be fully explored.

In 2000, the site of Tiwanaku was added to the United Nations Educational, Scientific and Cultural Organization (UNESCO) World Heritage List. The World Heritage List forms the framework for international cooperation in preserving and protecting cultural treasures and natural areas throughout the world.

"pagan" land should be divided between Portugal and Spain. Inspired by the pope's message, adventurers and soldiers set off to seek their fortunes in the New World.

In 1532 Francisco Pizarro and Diego de Almagro, two Spanish adventurers, arrived at the Incan capital with just 170 soldiers. They found an empire facing serious political problems. The sudden death of the Lord Inca had left the leadership of the empire in doubt, and a civil war had broken out between two sons of the Inca, Huáscar and Atahualpa.

According to some Spanish chroniclers of the period, the Incan nobility was amazed by these strange, white-skinned, bearded men who rode on horses as if joined to the animals. The Incas, as shown in these chronicles, had presumed that the conquistadores had been sent by the gods to settle the turmoil in the empire. As such, the Spaniards met little resistance.

The Spaniards arranged a meeting with the victorious Atahualpa and imprisoned him. Although the Incas paid a huge ransom in gold and silver to get their leader back, the Spanish executed him and took over the empire.

The last Inca emperor, Atahualpa, kneels before the Spanish conquistador Francisco Pizarro in this illustration from the 1500s.

SILVER

In 1544, Diego Huallpa, a native herder, lost some llamas in the region near the present-day city of Potosí. Unable to find them, he set up camp and lit a fire to keep warm. To his surprise the earth beneath his fire started to flow in a stream of molten metal. Huallpa had discovered silver. This subsequently brought thousands of settlers to South America. By 1650 the town of Potosí had a population of 160,000 and was one of the greatest cities in the Americas. The silver mined from the Cerro Rico ("Rich Mountain") was taken to the coast on the backs of llamas. From there Spanish galleons ferried it across the Atlantic to Europe.

For two hundred years the silver mines of Potosí paid the Spanish Empire's bills. According to local folklore, the Spanish took enough silver to build a bridge all the way to Spain.

The miners descended into the shafts by ropes, worked twelve-hour shifts by candlelight, and were kept underground for days or weeks. Thousands died each year from disease, ill treatment, and accidents. Most of the work was done by indigenous peoples brought in from all over the Andes. African slaves were imported, but few survived the cold. The mines were so feared that mothers deliberately crippled their sons so they would not be conscripted. It was at this time that the Spanish began to encourage the miners to chew coca leaves to help them endure the wretched conditions. Coca had previously been reserved for Incan priests and royalty.

La Paz was founded in 1548 as a staging point between the mines and the sea and soon became a major city. Oruro was the site of a second major silver find. Upper Peru, as Bolivia was then called, was soon one of the wealthiest corners of the Spanish Empire, and in 1559 a local government, the Audiencia of Charcas, was established under the control of the viceroy of Peru. The government was based in Chuquisaca, which became the political and educational center of the colony.

Many of the Spanish turned to farming and became the new land-owning aristocracy. Because the Spaniards took the best land, the indigenous peoples were pushed higher up the mountains, where they lived as tenant farmers, forced to work for the new owners.

Historical hero Túpac Katari was honored in 2013 when the Bolivian government named a telecommunications satellite after him.

Within two years, much of Incan society had been destroyed, and Pizarro and Almagro had divided South America between themselves. What is now Bolivia was ruled by Almagro and became known as Upper Peru or Charcas. Almagro's new wealth did him little good; he was assassinated by fellow Spaniards in 1538.

SPAIN DECLINES

The 1770s were a troubled time. After years of mistreatment, the indigenous population rebelled. The most notable of these revolts was led by Túpac Katari and his wife Bartolina Sisa, who, in 1781, led a great siege against La Paz from the highland above. Katari and Sisa set up court in El Alto and their army maintained the siege for 184 days, from March to June and from August to October.

The rebels were eventually captured and executed. Then there was an economic crisis. Between 1803 and 1825, silver production fell by 80 percent. By 1846, ten thousand mines had been abandoned.

In Upper Peru unrest was growing among the Creoles (South American-born people of Spanish parents). Having played a major part in building Spain's American empire, they were angry that top government positions were reserved for only those born in Spain.

French emperor Napoleon Bonaparte's conquest of Spain in 1808 gave the colonies the perfect opportunity to rebel. In 1809, Creoles in Chuquisaca (today's Sucre) and La Paz declared that they would recognize the exiled Spanish king but not the governors sent by the French.

On July 16, rebels in La Paz imprisoned the governor and elected Pedro Domingo Murillo president. The Spanish viceroy in Lima sent an army and quickly crushed the revolution. Nevertheless, a series of conflicts broke out across Spanish America from 1808 to 1833, all with the aim of breaking free of Spanish rule. In Upper Peru (today's Bolivia), the rebels fled to the hills and carried out a guerrilla campaign that lasted sixteen years. Ironically, Upper Peru, which had started the revolution in South America, was the last colony to gain its freedom.

THE FIGHT FOR FREEDOM

In 1814 in Europe, Napoleon was defeated and the Spanish monarchy restored, but South America had cultivated a taste for freedom, and the fight went on.

Simón Bolívar was a leading figure in this struggle. In a series of brilliant military campaigns, he brought independence to Venezuela, Colombia, and Ecuador. In 1824 he sent his revolutionary army to liberate Peru and bring colonial rule in South America to an end. Marshal Antonio José de Sucre was in charge of the campaign and won victories at Junín on August 6 and at Ayacucho on December 9 of the same year.

Historically, Upper Peru had always been linked with Lima, but that city had only just been freed from Spanish rule and there was no government in place. Many of the officers who had supported Sucre, particularly those who had deserted from the royalist army, wanted Upper Peru to be independent. Bolívar himself was against the idea and wanted the decision to wait until a new congress was formed in Lima. However, in February 1825, Sucre declared that Upper Peru must decide its own future, and on August 6, exactly a year after the first decisive battle, Upper Peru became an independent country, with Sucre as its first president.

Shortly afterward the new nation adopted the name Bolivia in honor of the great freedom fighter, and the city of Chuquisaca, where independence had been declared, became known as Sucre.

LOSING GROUND

Although the new South American nations had gained their independence, their borders were not clearly defined. As a result, Bolivia was dragged into a series of disastrous wars that resulted in the loss of large parts of its territory.

BOLÍVAR: THE GREAT FREEDOM FIGHTER

Simón Bolívar was born in Caracas, Venezuela, in 1783. His father died when Bolívar was three, and his mother died six years later. As was usual for young men from upper-class South American families, he was sent to Spain to complete his education. He married the daughter of a Spanish nobleman and brought her back to South America. She died of yellow fever only a few months after arriving in her new home.

Bolívar visited Europe again in 1804. During his time there he was inspired by the works of Enlightenment thinkers and writers, such as Voltaire, who advocated for civil liberties, progress, reason, and tolerance. It was then that the idea of an independent South America took hold of his imagination.

He returned to his homeland and joined the growing independence movement, which in 1810 expelled the Spanish governor from Caracas. Bolívar was sent to London, where he tried unsuccessfully to win British support for the struggle. He sailed back to South America, but when the revolution was crushed by troops loyal to Spain, he had to flee the country. While in exile in Cartagena, Colombia, in 1812, he wrote his most important political work, El Manifesto de Cartagena *(The Cartegena Manifesto).*

In 1819, Bolívar marched his army across the snow-covered Andes and took the Spanish army by surprise. He won a series of brilliant military victories and became president of the newly independent nation of Gran Colombia (roughly covering present-day Colombia, Panama, Venezuela, and Ecuador). In 1824, his army, under the command of Antonio José de Sucre, crushed the last Spanish royalists in Ecuador and Peru.

Bolívar had the vision of uniting all of South America into one great nation and was disillusioned when the continent broke up into a collection of independent countries. He became unpopular as a leader and was nearly assassinated. He resigned as president of Gran Colombia and died in 1830, at the age of forty-seven, worn out from a lifetime of fighting. Nevertheless, to many South Americans he will always be the legendary El Libertador.

The first blow came sixty years after independence. Bolivia owned land on the coast that was rich with nitrates and guano (bird droppings used for fertilizer), but Bolivia was not in a position to exploit these resources. Instead, Bolivia gave Chile permission to develop them. A dispute developed over what taxes the Chileans should pay for this concession, and this led to war in 1879, in which British fertilizer companies had a hidden hand.

Even though Peru came to Bolivia's aid, the Bolivian army was crushed at the Battle of Tacna. Bolivia played little part in the rest of the War of the Pacific and watched while Chile devastated Peru and took over a large part of Bolivian territory, including its access to the sea. Even today, Bolivia's relationship with Chile is shadowed by the question of sea access.

The war discredited Bolivia's military leaders, and this allowed the rich mine owners to gain power. Around this time mining started to recover from its earlier slump. The price of silver rose, and production increased as a result of investment in new equipment. In addition, industrialization in the West created a demand for tin, of which Bolivia had vast reserves.

THE CHACO WAR

Bolivia had a liberal government from 1899 to 1920 and enjoyed one of the calmest periods in its history. World War I in Europe brought new demands for tin, but although demand was high, the price remained low.

In 1932, a border dispute with Paraguay developed. The two nations are separated by the Gran Chaco, a desert plain that no one had been concerned about. By the 1930s, there were rumors of oil in the region, and the two nations started to argue over the position of the border. Bolivia set up a fort in the Chaco, which the Paraguayan army seized. Negotiations were taking place when the troops on the ground started fighting. The conflict escalated rapidly. Two oil companies, hoping to win rights to develop whatever oil was found, provided funds to cover the cost of the war: one backed Bolivia, while the other sided with Paraguay. Having just lost a war, Paraguay saw this as an opportunity to restore national pride.

The war lasted three years and ended in an armistice and a settlement in 1938. In a way, however, it was a defeat for Bolivia, because it lost the

Chaco and a huge number of people. As many as one hundred thousand Bolivians were either killed, wounded, or captured. At the end, Bolivia had lost another large part of its territory. Ironically, no oil was ever discovered in the disputed territory.

REVOLUTION AND REFORMS

The humiliating war convinced a new generation, called "the Chaco Generation," of the need for social and economic change. Calls for reform raised expectations of a better life, and leftist movements and political parties emerged—the most important being the *Movimiento Nacionalista Revolucionario* ("National Revolutionary Movement"), or MNR.

For many indigenous Bolivians who had fought in the war, the experience provided their first taste of being part of a nation as opposed to just being part of a local community. Thanks to the political conscience they gained, many participated in social movements in the years following the Chaco War.

The MNR drew support from mine workers and peasants to win the 1951 election, but the military, backed by conservatives, prevented the MNR's candidate, Víctor Paz Estenssoro, from taking power. Social unrest grew as the economy deteriorated, and militants staged a hunger march through La Paz that attracted a great deal of civilian support. The demoralized military began to fall apart and in April 1952, the MNR launched a rebellion that they easily won in only three days of fighting. Paz Estenssoro became president and introduced a range of reforms. Mines were nationalized, the indigenous population was given the right to vote, land laws were reformed, and primary education was introduced into the villages.

Despite these historic changes, the country continued to experience severe economic problems, and the MNR broke into a coalition of groups with different interests. Infighting within the party increased and the revolution lost its momentum. The MNR remained in power for twelve years before losing popularity due to its failure to improve the standard of living for the general population.

THE CATAVI MASSACRE

In December 1942, mine workers at the Catavi tin mine, along with those from the nearby Siglo XX mine, demanded an increase in wages. When management refused to negotiate, the miners' union called for a strike. The government quickly arrested all union leaders, and seven thousand miners went on strike. When the striking miners conducted a mass demonstration, the Bolivian military surrounded them and fired into the crowd for six hours. The official government report claimed nineteen deaths and four hundred wounded, while the workers themselves reported up to four hundred deaths.

A statue honors the miners who were killed by government troops at Catavi.

INSTABILITY

In 1964, there was a military coup. This marked the start of another period of instability, with one military government replacing another. During this time, the Argentine revolutionary Che Guevara was seeking to unite South America in fighting the widespread oppression of the poor by the power elite. In particular, he saw the root of the problem as the capitalist exploitation of Latin America by the United States. Indeed, the CIA was supporting a number of military dictatorships throughout South America at the time. In 1966, Guevara arrived in Bolivia to secretly build a guerrilla army in a remote area of the country. In October 1967, CIA operatives and the Bolivian army captured Guevara, and, on orders from President René Barrientos, executed him.

Years of instability followed, characterized by repeated coups, blatant election fraud, and strong-armed dictators. During the worst times, particularly the late 1970s, military leaders acting as president resorted to imprisoning and torturing their opponents in order to hang on to power. Dictators especially known for such practices were Generals Hugo Bánzer Suárez (dictator, 1971–1978, president, 1997–2001) and Luis García Meza (dictator, 1980–1981), but there were others as well.

Democracy was reestablished in 1982, at a moment when Latin America was entering an economic crisis. In 1985, Víctor Paz Estenssoro became president for the third time. He introduced some harsh economic reforms but managed to make both the political and economic situation more stable. During the 1990s, successive governments opened up Bolivia's market, paving the way for massive privatizations as part of a general strategy coordinated with international institutions to develop the economy and repay the country's enormous debt. In 1997, the former dictator Hugo Bánzer managed to win the presidency, becoming the first former dictator to transition successfully to democratic politics and legally return to power by way of the ballot box.

Bolivian President Victor Paz Estenssoro *(right)* is honored by England's Prince Philip in 1962.

INDIGENOUS PEOPLE POWER

Failure to improve the living conditions for many Bolivians, as well as the dismantling of many social services, the controversy over coca policies, and the selling off of natural resources led to social conflicts, street protests, and ultimately a profound political crisis. "Water war" demonstrations against water privatization in Cochabamba in 2000 were followed in 2003 by the "gas war" conflicts over the government's economic policies regarding natural gas. Both conflicts resulted in civilian deaths at the hands of the Bolivian armed forces, and both helped to galvanize the country's majority indigenous population to fight for political power.

THE WATER WAR

In 2000, a protest in the mountain city of Cochabamba turned into a deadly confrontation that came to be known as the Water War. The Bolivian government, then led by President Hugo Bánzer, had agreed to privatize all public enterprises (including mines, oil refineries, and utilities that had been nationalized after the revolution) in return for a $138 million loan from the World Bank. This included Cochabamba's local water system, which the government awarded to the sole bidder, Aguas del Tunari, a multinational consortium of private investors. The major shareholder was a subsidiary of the US-based Bechtel Corporation. The company won a forty-year concession to provide improved water and sanitation services to the residents of Cochabamba.

When the water company raised water delivery rates by 93 percent, and state water subsidies were simultaneously eliminated (as required by the World Bank), residents of Cochabamba protested. Riot police fired on demonstrators and the clash became violent. Protesters accused the Bechtel Corporation of "leasing the rain," and declared that water is a human right, not a commodity. The revolt spread to other communities. The government responded by arresting the leaders of the water protest. In April 2000, President Banzer declared a "state of siege," and a Bolivian army officer opened fired into a crowd of demonstrators, killing a seventeen-year-old boy. Further protests resulted in more deaths.

The company eventually pulled out; although it sued the Bolivian government for $25 million in compensation (the suit was later withdrawn). Cochabamba took control of its own water. However, without investment capital, the city has been unable to improve its aging system.

EVO MORALES

As a coca farmer and leader of the coca-growers union, Evo Morales (b. 1959) found himself in opposition to the Bolivian government early on. In the 1990s, Bolivia was cooperating with the United States in trying to eradicate coca as part of the US War on Drugs. Morales saw this as an example of continuing US intrusion in the affairs of Latin America, and more specifically, as an arrogant, tone-deaf rejection of indigenous Andean culture.

Morales soon expanded his interests beyond coca. In 1998, he helped found the political party Movement for Socialism (MAS) and became its leader.

When he was elected president in 2005, Morales became the first fully indigenous president in all of Latin America. He took office promising to bring full equality to Bolivia's indigenous people. To that end, he had a new constitution drawn up, which was approved in a national referendum in 2009 by a margin of 61.4 percent. He nationalized the country's natural resources. Adopting a policy known as "Coca Yes, Cocaine No," his administration legalized coca farming, but introduced regulations to oversee its production and trade.

Morales allied himself politically with Venezuela's president, the late Hugo Chávez, Brazil's Lula da Silva, and Cuba's Fidel Castro, thereby aligning Bolivia with the so-called "pink tide," or leftist, nations of Latin America. This has set the Morales administration at odds with the United States, a relationship that was not improved when Morales expelled the US diplomat Philip Goldberg in 2008. Morales also ordered the US Drug Enforcement Administration and its agents out of Bolivia, accusing the US officials of supporting his opposition and conspiring to overthrow him.

Morales is widely credited with instituting socio-economic reforms that have significantly lowered poverty rates in Bolivia. The unmarried, soccer-playing president remains extremely popular; however, some of the compromises he has made have caused disenchantment from the far left. Critics charge his government with corruption and a concentration of power. Meanwhile, wealthier and more conservative Bolivians are losing patience with Morales's long-lasting regime.

One of the active participants in the water and gas disputes was the Aymara labor leader Evo Morales, a former coca farmer and an avowed socialist. In 2005, he became the first indigenous man to become president of Bolivia. He won reelection in 2009, and again in 2014. In 2015, Morales's backers were reportedly seeking to amend Bolivia's constitution to allow him to run for reelection yet again in 2020.

In 2010, in Resolution 64/292, the United Nations General Assembly recognized water and sanitation as a human right. It declared that all people have the right to "sufficient, safe, acceptable, physically accessible, and affordable" water for personal and domestic uses. The United Nations Development Program (UNDP) said water costs should not exceed 3 percent of household income.

INTERNET LINKS

www.bbc.com/news/world-latin-america-12166905
A profile of Evo Morales is provided by BBC News.

news.bbc.co.uk/2/hi/americas/country_profiles/1218814.stm
The BBC News timeline of Bolivian history traces key events from 1538 to 2012.

www.coha.org/a-brief-recent-history-of-bolivia-and-the-rise-of-president-morales
This article traces the history of Bolivian indigenous activist movements to the rise of Evo Morales.

www.donquijote.org/culture/bolivia/history/bolivian-independence
This site offers a brief overview of the history of Bolivian independence.

www.lonelyplanet.com/bolivia/history
Lonely Planet gives a comprehensive overview of Bolivian history.

GOVERNMENT

Both the Bolivian national flag and the flag of the Andean indigenous people fly outside the presidential palace.

3

THE PLURINATIONAL STATE OF Bolivia is a republic headed by a democratically elected president. The country's 2009 constitution, which officially changed the name of the Republic of Bolivia to the Plurinational State of Bolivia, defines the nation as a "social unitarian state." This same constitution declares Sucre to be the national capital and makes no mention of La Paz. Nevertheless, the presidential palace and the Plurinational Legislative Assembly are located in La Paz, making it the seat of government and the administrative capital.

The *Palacio Quemado* ("Burned Palace"), located in La Paz, is the official residence of the Bolivian president. Its nickname comes from an event in 1875 when it was burned almost to the ground during an uprising. It has been rebuilt and renovated several times since then, but the name stuck.

THE CONSTITUTION

Bolivia has had numerous constitutions in its history, reflecting its long, unstable past. In 2009, the seventeenth constitution came into effect, and continues to be operational as of 2016. This newest constitution was approved by 61.43 percent in a referendum which drew more than 90 percent of Bolivian voters to the polls.

WHAT IS A PLURINATIONAL STATE?

"Bolivia is constituted as a Unitary Social State of Plurinational Community-Based Law that is free, independent, sovereign, democratic, intercultural, decentralized, and with autonomies. Bolivia is founded in plurality and political, economic, juridical, cultural, and linguistic pluralism within the integration process of the country."

—Political Constitution of the Plurinational State of Bolivia, First Part, Title I, Chapter I, Article 1

The 2009 Bolivian constitution added the term "plurinational state" to the nation's formal name. Plurinational *is a word that is not found in many English-language dictionaries. It means something like "multicultural" or "multinational." It is defined as the coexistence of two or more national groups within a political body (or country) of peoples.*

The term means more than merely recognizing—or even celebrating—the existence of multiple cultures within one national culture. Rather, it sees the political identities of different groups on two levels: as both part of, and yet different from, the national identity. In a plurinational state, the idea of nationalism is plural; there is more than one nationality. Therefore, political power is decentralized. In practice, this gives different groups a degree of political autonomy. In Bolivia, this constitutional change shifts a certain amount of self-determination to the indigenous peoples; the constitution lays out the parameters of those powers.

The new constitution defines Bolivia as a secular nation, rather than a Catholic one, as it was before. It also declares Bolivia to be a "pacifist state" that rejects war, although it reserves the right to "legitimate defense." The constitution prohibits the installation of foreign military bases within the country.

It establishes a mixed economy of state, private, and communal ownership, and restricts private land ownership to a maximum of 12,400 acres (5,000 ha). Prior to the 1952 revolution, 92 percent of usable land was held by individual landlords owning huge estates, which meant the vast majority of people had no land at all. The constitution also declares natural resources to be the exclusive dominion of the Bolivian people, administered by the state. In other words, all natural resources, such as water and natural gas, are nationalized rather than being privately owned.

Regarding the growing of coca, the new constitution states, "The State shall protect native and ancestral coca as cultural patrimony, a renewable natural resource of Bolivia's biodiversity, and as a factor of social cohesion; in its natural state it is not a narcotic. Its revaluing, production, commercialization, and industrialization shall be regulated by law."

The new document also made numerous other changes to Bolivia's governmental structure and laws.

President Evo Morales won a controversial third term in 2014.

THE EXECUTIVE

The president is both the head of state and the head of government. The president and vice president are elected for five-year terms. They are elected by popular vote, with a presidential run-off provision introduced in 2009. The president selects a cabinet of ministers to help him or her run the country, and has the right to rule by decree. The president oversees the running of the country, including its security and defense; directs foreign policy; works with the legislature to make laws; enforces court decisions, designates certain high-ranking officials, such as the attorney general and military commanders; issues supreme decrees and resolutions; and exercises "maximum authority" over land reform. The constitution also assigns the president the duty of "creating and constructing ports," which is deemed critical to the landlocked nation.

In 2014, President Evo Morales of the Movement for Socialism (MAS) party was reelected with 61.4 percent of the vote after a controversial 2013 court ruling allowed him to run for a third term. His supporters are trying to change the constitution to allow him to run again in 2019.

THE LEGISLATURE

The Plurinational Legislative Assembly replaces the previous National Congress. It consists of two houses, a 130-member Chamber of Deputies and a thirty-six-member Senate. All senators and fifty-three deputies are elected by proportional representation, and seventy deputies are elected in individual districts. Seven seats in the Chamber of Deputies are reserved for indigenous representatives. All serve five-year terms. In 2015, nearly half of the legislature was made up of women.

THE JUDICIARY

In October 2011, Bolivia held its first judicial elections to choose members of the national courts by popular vote. Previously judges had been directly elected by the Congress. The vote was the first time that a Latin American country directly elected its highest judicial officials.

The move wasn't without controversy. Some opposition parties claimed that electing judges could "erode the independence of the judiciary" because the 114 candidates were chosen by the Legislative Assembly, which held a majority of MAS party members. Critics therefore urged voters to either abstain or leave the ballots blank. Nevertheless, the vote went forward and twenty-eight elected members and twenty-eight alternates were sworn in on January 3, 2011, in Sucre.

The Bolivian court system includes:

- the Constitutional Tribunal, which rules on the constitutionality of government or court actions. For example, in 2012, the Constitutional Tribunal struck down Article 162 of the penal code, which made it a crime to criticize a government official in the exercise of his or her office;
- the Supreme Tribunal of Justice;
- the Agrarian and Environmental Tribunal;
- the Judiciary Council, which oversees the conduct of courts and judges; and district and local courts. Rural native indigenous jurisdiction is exercised by their own authorities, and "ordinary" or state jurisdiction and rural native indigenous jurisdiction enjoy equal status.

THE ELECTORAL PROCESS AND POLITICAL PARTIES

Citizens of La Paz vote in the 2014 election.

The Plurinational Electoral Organ is an independent branch of the Bolivian government. Voting is universal and compulsory in Bolivia. The voting age is eighteen for all people. Before 1995, the voting age was eighteen for married people and twenty-one for singles. Prior to 1952, only literate people could vote, a move that naturally favored the aristocracy over the indigenous poor.

The country operates on a multiparty system, and citizens have the right to organize political parties. Since the election of Evo Morales and the MAS, the old parties have mostly collapsed and are being replaced by newer ones or coalitions. The MAS remains strong, however, and so far, opposition parties have not garnered the same level of popularity. In the 2014 election, Samuel Doria Medina of the National Unity Party won 24 percent of the vote, and Jorge Quioga of the Christian Democratic Party won only 9 percent. Morales's attempt to run for a fourth term, however, is already sparking a new level of opposition.

LOCAL GOVERNMENT AND AUTONOMY

Bolivia is divided into nine departments, each ruled by an elected prefect, or departmental governor. The departments are subdivided into provinces, which are controlled by subprefects. Provinces are divided into cantons. Cities and towns are governed by directly elected mayors and councils.

FLAG AND EMBLEM

The Bolivian flag, called La Tricolor *("the tricolor"), is divided into three horizontal stripes of red, gold, and green. The flag flown on government buildings also includes the Bolivian coat of arms in the center of the gold band. This national emblem includes a condor, Mount Potosí, and a woolly alpaca. The red band in the flag represents the blood of the brave soldiers of the armed forces, the green is for fertility and the land, and the yellow stands for the nation's mineral wealth.*

In addition to the national flag, which dates to 1851, the 2009 constitution establishes the Wiphala (sometimes spelled whipala) as a dual flag of Bolivia. The square emblem represents the indigenous people of the Andes, including those in Peru, Ecuador, and parts of Argentina, Chile, and Colombia. This colorful emblem is often used as a flag. It consists of seven symbolic colors—red, orange, yellow, white, green, blue, and violet— arranged diagonally in a patchwork of forty-nine smaller squares. Both the Tricolor and the Wiphala fly outside the presidential palace in La Paz.

Attractive as it is, the Wiphala has caused much controversy in Bolivia since its official desgination. One reason is that it only represents the Andean indigenous, and not the native cultures of the other regions; and the white, mestizo, and other populations also feel excluded and view the new flag with some suspicion.

FOREIGN POLICY

There has not been a US ambassador in Bolivia since September 2008 when President Evo Morales expelled the ambassador and the US Drug Enforcement Agency from the country. Nevertheless, the US Embassy in La Paz remains in operation and Bolivia continues to maintain an embassy in Washington, DC. Drug policy is a particular sticking point, and the United States is also wary of the leftist nature of the current Morales administration.

On another front, one of landlocked Bolivia's greatest goals is to achieve access to the sea. This desire affects its foreign policy with neighboring countries, especially Chile. Bolivia maintains that it has sovereignty over territory that extends to the Pacific Ocean. The coastal land was taken from it in the War of the Pacific (1879–1883), a conflict between Bolivia, Chile, and Peru. Bolivia has taken its claim to the International Court of Justice in The Hague, which agreed in 2015 to hear the case. For its part, in 2015, Chile's foreign minister Heraldo Muñoz said his country would be willing to help Bolivia gain access to the sea across its territory, but that it could not agree to Bolivia's claim of sovereignty.

INTERNET LINKS

www.constituteproject.org/constitution/Bolivia_2009.pdf
This is a full English translation of Bolivia's constitution.

www.economist.com/news/americas/21650578-south-american-border-dispute-has-implications-international-law-beaches-future
This article explains the conflict and international court case involving Bolivia's attempt to gain sovereign access to the Pacific Ocean.

freedomhouse.org/report/freedom-world/2015/bolivia
This pro-democracy site gives an overview and evaluation of the Bolivian government.

ECONOMY

Quinoa has fed the Andean people for centuries but has recently become popular worldwide.

4

The United Nations General Assembly declared 2013 as the "International Year of Quinoa," in recognition of the Andean grainlike "super food." Bolivia is the world's top producer of quinoa, and at the official launch of the celebratory year, President Evo Morales said, "Quinoa is an ancestral gift of the Andean people."

DURING TIMES OF WORLDWIDE economic downturn in the past ten years, Bolivia has been a surprising bright spot. This struggling country, historically the poorest in South America, posted an average annual growth rate of 5 percent each year from 2005 to 2014, with a remarkable 6.8 percent rate in 2013. Even critics of President Evo Morales had to admit that at least some of the growth could be attributed to his policies. Despite this happy news, Bolivia remains far behind most of its Latin American neighbors. Whether this growth will continue into the next decade is a matter of conjecture, but some economists think it unlikely.

It may seem puzzling that a country with such a wealth of natural resources remains so impoverished. In 2015, Bolivia's gross domestic product (GDP) was very low at $3,124 per capita income, compared with $12,509 in Argentina and $54,629 in the United States. Many, perhaps most, Bolivians live below the poverty line.

SHOESHINE BOYS

Shoeshine boys are seen everywhere in Bolivian towns. Most are young boys, starting at six or seven years old, but old men also provide this service. Some have permanent chairs, almost like thrones, on which customers climb up, sit, and have their shoes polished while they read the newspaper. Other shoeshine boys carry all their equipment with them in small boxes and wait around park benches for customers. Some carry cell phones on which a customer can make a call for a small fee.

To some observers, shoeshine boys seem like an innocuous part of the landscape, but others consider this to be child labor. Boys who have not dropped out of school often wear masks to avoid being identified by their schoolmates. Many give most of their earnings to their underemployed parents. But some are homeless, sniff glue, and sleep on the streets.

There are various reasons why the country remains so poor, including the rugged landscape, which makes transportation and infrastructure development difficult, and the lack of a direct access to the sea. A lack of foreign investment has limited the development of Bolivia's economy; political instability has been a major factor, along with the lack of education and high incidence of disease among the workers. Bolivia has the highest percentage of indigenous population in South America, about two-thirds, and historical racism has kept them destitute.

NATURAL RESOURCES

Bolivia has considerable natural resources. In the past, international corporations extracted or processed the materials, sending the product and profits out of the country. In 2009, the new Bolivian constitution declared that the country's natural resources belong to the Bolivian people. This doesn't mean that no private firms can be employed in the business of processing those resources, or that the resources cannot be exported. Rather, it means that ownership of the natural materials themselves is nationalized and private companies work under service contracts negotiated by the state, which collects taxes and royalties. Today, gas and minerals together form about 73 percent of the country's exports.

Water resources abound, but have yet to be fully tapped. With its many mountains and rivers, Bolivia has considerable potential for producing hydroelectric power. The first projects were built in the vicinity of La Paz and Cochabamba. Meanwhile, however, as water resources are economically exploited, Bolivia needs to be mindful of environmental costs.

MINERALS Virtually every valuable mineral is found in Bolivia. In the past, the country relied heavily on the mining sector, especially silver and tin, to support its economy, but is now trying to diversify. It is a major world producer of bismuth, zinc, lead, and antimony. Gold and silver are also exported. Tin used to be the most important export. The fall in tin prices in the mid-1980s was devastating for Bolivia, where tin is expensive to extract. For every $2.50 the country was paid for tin, it spent $10 to mine and transport it. Many mines were closed and unemployment soared, as twenty thousand miners lost their jobs.

Today, the mining sector has declined, but the demand remains. In 2013, 17 percent of Bolivia's exports came from the mining sector. Some mines are state-run, others are cooperatives, and some are operated by international corporations—the largest being the Japanese Sumitomo Corporation, which runs the San Cristóbal mine. Mining will likely play an important role in Bolivia's economy for a long time to come. Meanwhile, vast, untapped lithium reserves may hold the key to its future economic growth.

OIL Another resource is oil. Bolivia's oil fields produce about 52,000 barrels a day, which meets most of its domestic demand. In 2014, it exported about

THE MINERS

Bolivia mines gold, silver, tin, and other minerals. Some mines are owned by the miners themselves and operated as cooperatives. Life is often hardest in these mines because there is little money to invest in equipment. Most of the work is done using hand tools, with miners working in narrow, unventilated, and unbearably hot passageways.

Although no one under the age of eighteen is supposed to work in the mines, boys age twelve or thirteen—or even younger—are sometimes taken on as helpers. After three or four years, they can apply to the cooperative to become miners.

Generally the miners gather early in the morning at the mine and linger outside, drinking tea and chewing coca to prepare themselves for the day ahead. Once underground they may work for nine hours before returning to the surface. Miners in cooperative mines set their own dynamite to loosen the rock. It can take two or three hours just to chisel out a hole for the dynamite. After the explosion the tunnel is full of dangerous fumes, and while waiting for these to disperse, the miners take a coca break. Miners believe that chewing coca not only gives them energy but also filters out some of the harmful fumes they breathe in.

All miners, whether in cooperative or state-owned mines, have a hard and dangerous job. Even if they are lucky enough to avoid accidents, working in the mines almost inevitably leads to serious lung disease, and many miners die before they reach fifty.

13,000 barrels of crude oil a day, with about half going to Argentina. Bolivia also imports refined petroleum products from Chile, Argentina, and the United States. The oil fields were first developed in the 1920s by the Standard Oil Company of Bolivia, a US—based company. The government took over the fields in 1937. Only after the 1952 revolution did the industry start to receive the investment capital it required.

NATURAL GAS Bolivia has the second-largest natural gas reserves in South America. Gas pipelines run into Argentina and Brazil, where most of it is exported. Gas has replaced tin as the top export commodity, and constitutes around 56 percent of Bolivia's exports.

Gas has become a major economic and political issue. In 2003 an uprising occurred when newly discovered natural gas fields were signed over for export to a multinational consortium. The country's poor, tired of seeing national resources exported without improvement to their own quality of living, erected blockades throughout the country. Gas exploitation was halted in what is now known as the "Gas War."

A "Second Gas War" in 2005, where people demanded nationalization, led to a new political crisis and elections. The new government has taken control of natural gas, but must attract the foreign investment needed to develop this important sector.

AGRICULTURE

Agriculture employs about 32 percent of Bolivians, yet Bolivia cannot grow sufficient food to feed its population. Farming is held back by antiquated methods. On the Altiplano, much of the work is still done by hand, and the poor soil barely provides sufficient food for each family to survive. There have been attempts both to modernize agriculture and to bring back some of the successful methods employed by the Incas on the same land.

The more fertile Yungas produce much of the food for La Paz and other cities. These warmer, more fertile areas grow a wider range of fruit and vegetables, including bananas, oranges, turnips, carrots, and cassava, as well as coffee. The Santa Cruz and Beni departments are cattle-ranching country.

QUINOA FOR HEALTH AND PROFIT

Not long ago, most people outside of South America had never heard of quinoa (KEEN-wha). The colorful grain was originally grown by Andean people thousands of years ago, and has been a key protein source for the people of that region ever since. The Inca called it the "mother of all grains" and considered it to be sacred. Outside of the Andes region, however, quinoa remained obscure; Spanish colonists shunned it as "Indian food" and for centuries it had a reputation as "food for poor people."

Bolivia is the world's top quinoa exporter. The plant grows in dry soil and cold temperatures and is highly adapted to the harsh conditions of the mountains and Altiplano. The grain is actually not a grain at all but a seed which can be cooked like rice or other cereals. Technically, it is a pseudocereal, like buckwheat and amaranth. There are many varieties, with seeds of white, black, red, and yellow. In its natural state, the seeds are covered with a bitter coating, which makes them unpalatable to birds. This coating must be washed off before cooking, and most commercial quinoa sold today has already been through that process.

In recent years, quinoa has been "discovered" by the rest of the world, and the market demand has skyrocketed. Its agreeable taste and high nutrient value has made it a good gluten-free substitute for other grains. This increase in popularity has been good for Bolivia's economy, which has grown significantly since 2005. However, analysts worry that overreliance on this one commodity could lead to disaster down the road. Also, it has had the unintended effect of making quinoa too expensive for the indigenous Andean people who rely on it.

The beef is largely for the domestic market, with some exported to Peru and Brazil.

Traditionally the rain forest has added little to the agricultural economy, except for Brazil nuts and latex. There is great potential for extracting tropical hard woods, causing growing conflict between loggers and environmentalists.

INDUSTRY

Because of the small population and the limited spending power of most of the people, Bolivia has only a small market for manufactured goods.

Much of Bolivian industry is still based in small- or medium-sized factories, which produce items to meet daily needs, including textiles, shoes, blankets, and pharmaceuticals. Two-thirds of factories in Bolivia are based in or around La Paz. Santa Cruz and Cochabamba are the other major industrial centers.

Larger factories have been set up to support the mining industry. There are also several oil refineries. Other factories use by-products from oil to produce a wide range of items.

Another important sector is food processing, particularly sugar, coffee, and rice. Several cities have large breweries, and local wine is also made in the south of the country.

Industry employs about 20 percent of the workforce, but a great deal of manufacturing takes place in small, family-run workshops employing only two or three people. Such places are seldom registered and operate outside the official figures.

In recent years many new industrial projects have begun operations. These range from a ceramic tile industry in Sucre to a new textile factory in Tarija that combines angora wool with cotton.

CHILD LABOR

In very impoverished nations, it's typical to find children working at tender ages, at least by Western standards. Official statistics are hard to come by, but a 2008 report estimated that about eight hundred thousand children

COCA, BOLIVIA'S CONTROVERSIAL CROP

Coca—not to be confused with cacao, the cocoa bean—is a plant that figures mightily in Bolivia's culture, history, and politics. Indigenous Bolivians have been chewing coca leaves and drinking coca tea for many centuries, and the plant has traditionally been valued for its medicinal, nutritional, and religious applications. The plant's leaves contain an alkaloid, or naturally occurring chemical compound, which has psychotropic, or mind-altering, qualities. The alkaloid in coca is cocaine. When ingested, it changes brain function and can effect perception, mood, or consciousness.

The alkaloid content of coca leaves is relatively low, so chewing the leaves or drinking coca tea does not produce the same effects that people experience by using cocaine. Natural coca also doesn't cause addiction. In Bolivia, using coca in these ways is legal and an important part of Andean culture.

Whatever the merits of coca itself, when its alkaloid is extracted and made into cocaine, it becomes a dangerous drug. Extracting the cocaine from coca is done through a chemical process involving several solvents. Most Bolivian coca grows in the Yungas and the Chapare region of North Cochabamba. Coca from the Yungas is used domestically, but the Chapare crop is sometimes shipped to laboratories hidden deep in the rain forest, where it is turned into cocaine. This is sent to Colombia, the center of international cocaine-trafficking rings. From there it is smuggled into the United States and Europe.

Coca eradication programs partly financed by the United States during different governments in the late 1990s led to a near complete stoppage of Chapare coca exports. However, the market for it in the United States and Europe remained strong, so coca production merely shifted to Colombia. Coca farmers, many of them former miners who were laid off, were never given viable markets for alternative agricultural products and have thus become even more impoverished.

Since the election of President Evo Morales, a former coca grower, the government has taken a new approach to coca growing that legalizes the coca leaf for legal products while outlawing cocaine.

worked in Bolivia. Of that, 491,000 were under the age of fourteen. That works out to about one in four children.

In 2014, Bolivia passed a new law that essentially lowered the working age to ten. This measure drew condemnation from many critics, including the United Nations Children Fund (UNICEF). However, Bolivian officials said it is part of a plan to eradicate extreme poverty by 2025.

The new measure keeps the official working age at fourteen, which is widely considered acceptable in developing countries. It makes some exceptions, however, which recognize a truth in the country, which is that younger children are already working, legally or not. According to the new law, children age ten to twelve are allowed to work if they attend school, are self-employed, and get parental permission. Age twelve and above, children can do light work for others. Mining and brick making—where child labor is rampant—are not considered "light work." In all cases, the work needs to be authorized and registered with a child protection officer. Whether the new law will prove beneficial or even enforceable remains to be seen.

INTERNET LINKS

www.aljazeera.com/indepth/features/2012/09/201292775351464532.html
"Bleak Life in Dark Bolivian Mine" is an article about a child miner.

www.aljazeera.com/indepth/features/2015/09/bolivia-stands-coca-control-policy-150930085832276.html
This article provides a good overview of coca production in Bolivia under new government policies.

www.bbc.com/news/business-30117126
This article is "Child labour laws: A step back for advancing Bolivia?"

www.fao.org/quinoa-2013/press-room/news/detail/en
This is the home page of the UN International Year of Quinoa.

ENVIRONMENT

Bolivia's heavily mined Cerro Rico has been called "the mountain that eats men."

5

IN ANCIENT TIMES MOUNTAINS AROSE, rivers moved, and lakes were formed. Our Amazonia, our swamps, our highlands, and our plains and valleys were covered with greenery and flowers. We populated this sacred Mother Earth with different faces, and since that time we have understood the plurality that exists in all things and in our diversity as human beings and cultures."

So begins the Preamble to Bolivia's 2009 constitution. By calling attention to the land itself as the foundation from which the nation grew, the document underscores the importance of the environment in Bolivia's identity.

Bolivia's Andean and tropical environment remains one of the least damaged in the world. The more remote corners of this vast and underpopulated country are hardly touched by human activity. Ironically, because so much has survived, there is much to protect.

Threats to the environment come in many forms: from the differing values of different classes of people; from inside the country; or from abroad. Whether the motivation is profit or survival, it is Mother Earth, what many Bolivians refer to as the Pachamama, which pays the price. It is more than wildlife, water, or glaciers that are at stake; it's the lives of people and the existence of whole cultures and ways of life.

Cerro Rico ("Rich Mountain"), the peak pictured at the center of the Bolivian flag, is in danger of collapse from excessive silver mining, which has continued since the sixteenth century. The vast complex of mining tunnels has left the mountain unstable, yet mining continues. The summit has already developed a giant sinkhole. A UNESCO World Heritage site, it was added to the list of World Heritage in Danger in 2014.

PROTECTED AREAS

Torotoro National Park features deep canyons such as this one.

In Bolivia there are dozens of national parks or reserves spread out around the country. While the definition of a protected area can be debated, at least 15 percent and as much as 35 percent of Bolivia's territory is "protected." Access to such areas is often difficult. Indeed, during the rainy season, floods cause communications to be blocked, making it hard to reach many areas within national parks.

The fate of these parks has sometimes led to conflicts. Restricted portions of the protected territory have been granted to local farmers or small entrepreneurs who want to use their resources. However, the government often finds it difficult to enforce anti-encroachment laws against people with no such permission to operate in the protected regions. There have also been conflicts with oil companies wanting to exploit parts of the reserves that are the traditional homes of indigenous peoples.

Many national parks are open to visitors. For example there is Torotoro National Park, in the Andes, where rock formations and more than 2,500 dinosaur prints can be seen. The Cotapata Park, in the Yungas region near La Paz, contains the famous Incan trail, called the Choro. There, hikers can trek downward from the Andes to more tropical areas. Visitors can find misty lagoons in Eduardo Avaroa Park and, in Sajama Park, the snowcapped Sajama volcano, the highest peak in Bolivia. Many parks, including Amboró and Madidi, are the natural habitats of an incredibly wide variety of wildlife.

Bolivia held its first ever National Day of Protected Areas on September 4, 2005. The aim of this annual event is to raise awareness among Bolivians about what a protected area is and how it can benefit the country.

THREATENED SPECIES

Bolivia owes its diversity of plant and animal life to the unparalleled variety of landscapes, from the Andes highlands to the Amazon lowlands. This is home to a great number of endemic animals and plants, meaning species not found anywhere else in the world. At least seventy-nine vertebrates and four thousand vascular plants exist only in Bolivia, with new species being discovered each year by expeditions of scientists and students.

While many criticize Bolivia's lack of development of a road network, which are so essential to economic growth, this is likely what has protected much of the diversity of wildlife that exists in the country. However, this does not prevent many species from being threatened. It can be debated when a species should be considered threatened, and there tends to be a hierarchy of factors for determining which species are the most endangered, leading to categories such as "critically endangered," "endangered," and "vulnerable species."

Bolivia is home to 361 mammal species, 1,414 bird species, 258 reptile species, and 161 amphibian species. Of these, 26 mammal species, 30 bird species, two reptile species, and 21 amphibian species are endangered. Such animals are often threatened by hunters looking for food or for illegal trade. Many specimens of these species, including hyacinth macaws, baby capuchin monkeys, and ocelots, end up as pets, even if it is illegal to keep them in captivity. Bolivian authorities lack resources and determination to apply and enforce laws on protection of wild animals.

Of the identified 17,367 species of plants in the country, 70 are at risk. In addition, 70 of Bolivia's 2,700 species of native trees are threatened. Uncontrolled farming and logging, as well as urbanization, are some of the causes of species endangerment.

DEFORESTATION

Deforestation is considered a problem in Bolivia precisely because so many forested ecosystems have survived in this land, most notably the beautiful cloud forests, which are rare in any part of the world. Some 70 percent of Bolivia's land mass is part of the Amazon River basin, from biodiverse foothills to lowland jungles. Every year, nearly 1,400 square miles (3,626 sq km) are deforested, about two-thirds the size of Delaware.

Illegal loggers can carry on their business in relative secrecy ironically because of this successful protection of nature, for they can penetrate deep into forests far from any human vigilance. This illegal trade is

This aerial view shows the clear cutting of the Amazon forest in the eastern lowlands of Bolivia.

partly responsible for increasing degrees of deforestation, especially with the exploitation of the endangered hardwood called big-leafed mahogany. No such economy can remain in business without a consumer base, and much of this illegal wood finds its way to US consumers. This one hardwood accounts for more than 50 percent of US imports of tropical wood, and 18 percent of such mahogany imports come from Bolivia. In 2011, the Convention on International Trade in Endangered Species (CITES) shut down Bolivia's mahogany exports, due to lack of oversight.

Given consumer thirst for this product and an impoverished local population in need of the income, government crackdowns on such illegal timber production were largely ineffective. Newer programs attempt to create sustainable models of forest exploitation, such as those sponsored by the World Wildlife Fund and the International Finance Corporation. These and other programs attempt to show loggers that it is in their own best interest to not destroy the very forest that is supporting them. The loss of forests would contribute to other environmental tragedies, such as desertification and the loss of endemic animal and plant species.

The other major factor contributing to deforestation is known as slash-and-burn agriculture, mainly occurring in tropical rain forests. In the 1960s when development was needed, the Bolivian government offered free 75- to 125-acre (30 to 50 ha) plots of land to migrants to clear and farm. But once rain forest land is cleared, the rains wash away the fertile soils. After two or three harvests the land is no longer worth farming, and these "shifting cultivators" must move to another parcel of land.

Agriculture specialists are attempting to develop a more sustainable agriculture that would permit farming families to remain in the same place and not ravage the surrounding scrublands and forests. Recent experiments with cover crops (those that protect the soil against runoff and provide fertilizing nutrients) attempt to minimize the effects of soil erosion. Farmers in the rain forests and valleys have been using leguminous plants as cover crops. Lowland farmers that were once "shifting cultivators" now have the chance to remain on their fixed plots by rotating rice and bean crops to replenish nitrogen in the soil for the next season of rice.

Some environmentalists challenge whether there is indeed such a thing as "sustainable" logging or agriculture in such rich forests, but until the Bolivian economy creates other job opportunities, pragmatic solutions seem to be the only alternative currently in practice.

About one-fifth of Bolivia's territory is classified as legally conserved, one of the highest rates in the world. It could be argued that the oxygen that these forests provide to the rest of the world is worth some type of compensation. The forests of developed countries, such as those in Europe and North America, have already been largely decimated by development. Thus farmers and loggers in poorer countries consider the arguments of developed countries against their economy to be hypocritical.

WATER POLLUTION

Water pollution is another form of assault upon the environment. A sad example is the damage done to the Choqueyapu River in La Paz. Situated in a valley, La Paz is full of surface and underground streams, which converge into the Choqueyapu. While in the past it was possible to bathe in its water, rapid urbanization and industrialization have turned it into an open sewer. Millions of tons of human litter and industrial and organic waste are emptied into the river each year.

Though a part of the river-turned-sewer is now covered, much of it is still an ugly sight and smell to people passing by that part of the city. Even in the rich neighborhoods, people have to live with the contamination of the Choqueyapu. As is often the case, the poor people suffer the most from the pollution. Aside from the obvious threat of diseases, many poor people live near the river and use its water to wash clothes or water crops, among other things. Conceivably, residue of the river pollution can find its way onto the fruits and vegetables sold in markets.

One major cause of water pollution is mining. Often those exploiting mines pay little attention to the environmental consequences. This is what happened with the Pilcomayo River. Water pollution caused by runoff from the mines resulted in poor harvests and high cattle mortality in the region, leading to protests from local farmers. Investigations revealed that there is indeed a high level of contamination around mines, more than what is legally allowed, and some companies have been put on trial.

Small-scale mining is another source of pollution. Ever since the massive layoffs of miners beginning in 1985, some unemployed miners turned to coca growing, while many others joined small and primitively operated mining cooperatives, especially in places where gold might be found. Much of this mining is not regulated by the government, and environmental norms are not respected, which not only leads to negative consequences on miners' health, but also on the environment. This activity causes the emission of tons of mercury each year, an extremely toxic element that first affects rivers and eventually reaches the food chain. Possible solutions include alternative methods for extracting gold, but such methods remain underutilized.

CLIMATE CHANGE

Bolivia is the highest elevation country in South American and temperatures in the Andes have been rising since 1975. The glacier of Mount Chacaltaya lost half of its area and two-thirds of its volume during the last century, and the process is accelerating. This affects the ecosystem since it is the Andean glaciers that largely feed the Amazon rain forest. A 2008 report predicted that climate change could eliminate enough glaciers in the Andes by 2028 to threaten the existence of 100 million people in surrounding countries, all due to the loss of the annual water flow from the melted glaciers. Indeed, in 2016, Lake Poopó, the country's second largest lake, dried up completely.

At the high elevations of Andean villages, rising temperatures are affecting traditional agriculture. Certain plants that thrived in the cooler temperatures are failing in warmer ones. Insects that previously could not survive at those altitudes are now causing infestations.

In October 2015, Bolivia hosted a three-day climate change conference that was attended by five thousand people from more than forty countries. President Evo Morales used the occasion to criticize both the United States and capitalism for contributing to climate change but doing too little to address it.

A fisherman walks along the abandoned boats in the dried up Lake Poopó in January 2016.

INTERNET LINKS

news.mongabay.com/2015/08/identidad-madidi-major-expedition-in-bolivian-national-park-discovers-new-species
This article has many beautiful images of Bolivia's Madidi National Park and the extraordinary species that live there.

www.npr.org/2012/09/06/160171565/guess-whos-chopping-down-the-amazon-now
Bolivia's deforestation situation is discussed in this article.

www.nytimes.com/2009/12/14/science/earth/14bolivia.html
The *New York Times* presents the article, "In Bolivia, Water and Ice Tell of Climate Change."

www.pbslearningmedia.org/resource/ess05.sci.ess.earthsys.bolivia/deforestation-in-bolivia
This graphic, in video or slide show format, is a powerful visual presentation of Bolivia's deforestation since 1984.

BOLIVIANS

A young Aymara farmer shows off his calf.

6

BOLIVIANS ARE A MULTIETHNIC, multiracial, and multilingual people. According to the new 2009 constitution, when the country's official name became the Plurinational State of Bolivia, they are also, in a sense, a multinational people. They are made up of multiple human communities and identities which reflect the region's long history.

Indigenous people are descendents of various South American pre-Columbian cultures, primarily those of the Andes region. *Mestizos* ("mixed") are people of both white European (mainly Spanish) and indigenous descent. Of course, there are other kinds of mixed-race people, but in Bolivia, the word *mestizo* refers exclusively to a white/indigenous ethnicity. Bolivians also include a minority of white people, most of whom claim direct Spanish descent; and also people of African and Asian descent. By far, the majority of Bolivians are indigenous or mestizo. Exact figures are difficult to report because native identities often overlap, and census reports have used different terminologies over the years. One report claims some 60 percent of Bolivians to be indigenous, with about 30 percent being mestizo; while a more recent report reverses those figures. It's safe to say that about 80 to 90 percent of Bolivians are indigenous or mestizo, between 5 and 10 percent are white, and about 1 percent are black. Other groups are smaller.

Bolivia once had a reputation of providing a safe haven for Nazi war criminals. Although many stories of war crimes are based on rumors, Klaus Barbie, a Nazi Gestapo chief who conducted a reign of terror in southern France, lived in Bolivia for several years. With the participation of the Bolivian government, he was finally extradited to France to face a sentence of life imprisonment. He died in 1991.

Bolivians number about 10,800,900, which is not a large amount for a country so vast. There are slightly fewer people in Bolivia than in Ohio. However, the population is not evenly distributed. The lowland plains are less heavily populated, while most Bolivians live on the Altiplano. About 68.5 percent live in urban areas.

The lowland people tend to reflect the warm, sunny weather of their region, with their informal and lively behavior. They usually wear brighter colors and lighter clothes and have the reputation of being the liveliest dancers. Generally thought of as being more adventurous, they also tend to be more business oriented.

Highlanders tend to be conservative and reserved. People from La Paz, for example, are more cautious in their dress and behavior and speak more slowly. Experts from different disciplines have not been able to explain why this highland-lowland dichotomy exists throughout Latin America.

THE INDIGENOUS HIGHLANDERS

Bolivia's indigenous highlanders are a rugged, strong-spirited people who have retained much of their culture and identity. The two main groups are the Aymara and the Quechua.

Both groups have slightly larger lungs than average, enabling them to take in more oxygen, and extra blood vessels in their limbs to help keep them warm. The Quechua mainly live in the south of the Altiplano, around Cochabamba, Sucre, and Potosí. The Aymara farm the land around La Paz and Lake Titicaca. The two seldom mix, and intermarriage is rare.

Many from both groups have left the countryside to seek work in cities. Initially the breaking of family ties led to problems from alcohol abuse. People have since adjusted, and the second and third generations, with the advantage of education, have set higher goals in their personal and social struggles to improve their condition.

Although native labor was always important to the economy, indigenous people remain isolated from dominant social sectors. Only since the 1952 revolution have there been attempts to change this, and only in 1975 were Quechua and Aymara made official languages.

THE QUECHUA The Quechua are spread across Peru, Bolivia, and Ecuador. Traditionally they lived in isolated agricultural communities. Recently many have moved to cities to find employment, particularly in construction. The urban Quechua are likely to be bilingual and their lifestyle less traditional.

In more isolated rural communities, the traditional home is a small, one-room building made of sun-dried bricks and a thatched roof. A hearth stands in one corner for the fire. The main highland crop is potatoes, and their livestock usually includes llamas. In valleys the crops are more varied, with corn as a staple. The llamas are rarely slaughtered but are occasionally sold when money is needed. Their wool is woven into shawls and ponchos, which the women weave on traditional peg looms. The family might also keep an alpaca, but its internationally popular wool is more likely to be sold than used for the family.

A Quechua woman sells different types of quinoa at a market in Salinas de Garci Mendoza. The town is called the "Capital of Quinoa."

Looking after the animals is usually the job of the youngest children, who are put to work as soon as they can walk. After the age of eleven or twelve, the task of looking after livestock is passed on to younger siblings, and the older children start to help their parents in the fields.

THE AYMARA The Aymara probably arrived at Lake Titicaca sometime between 1400 and 400 BCE. It is likely they came from central Peru, although their arrival in this region is an unsolved historical mystery. They were a fiercely independent people and were able to retain their language after being conquered by the Incas.

The Aymara defend their traditions, and life in rural areas is similar to what it must have been like one thousand years ago. A typical rural home is built from mud bricks and is either a one-room building or a two-story house. There are likely to be some outbuildings, and the whole complex might be surrounded by a mud-brick wall. A few roofs are still thatched, but corrugated metal is now widely used. Cooking and washing are done outside.

The Aymara grow barley, potatoes, quinoa, beans, onions, and garlic. In the warmer valleys many also produce corn and fruit. Many supplement their diet, or earn a living, from fishing.

A Kallawaya man wears the traditional hat, which each man knits for himself.

THE KALLAWAYA The Kallawaya come from the eastern shore of Lake Titicaca. They are probably related to the Aymara, although their origins are unclear. Legend claims they are direct descendants of the Tiwanaku who lived there by 800 CE.

The Kallawaya are farmers and traveling healers. The healers are knowledgeable about the medicinal properties of herbs, using a multitude of plants to effect their cures. The Kallawaya also use spells, charms, and music as holistic aids in their therapies.

The Kallawaya ability to cure is respected throughout Bolivia, and Kallawaya healers can be found all over the country. Several foreign scientists are now studying Kallawaya methods. For the Kallawaya, sickness and disease occur when there is an imbalance of *ajallu* (ah-HAH-yu), or life force.

Because of their nomadic lifestyle, Kallawaya healers tend to be multilingual, able to speak various indigenous dialects as well as Spanish. In addition they have their own "secret" language. A legend claims that because of their healing skills, the Kallawaya were taken to the Incan capital and still speak the language of the ancient royal court.

THE CHIPAYA The Chipaya live in one of the most remote parts of the Altiplano, around Coipasa Salt Field. Nobody is sure why they moved to such an inhospitable area, but today's Chipaya claim the Aymara stole their lands. They now number fewer than 2,000 and mostly live in one village. The Chipaya look similar to the Aymara but generally have broader faces and darker skin.

They tend to wear rough-looking cloth of beige, brown, and black. Chipaya women are easily distinguished by the way they wear their hair in hundreds of small braids.

The Chipaya subsist by farming and herding llamas and sheep. Unlike the Aymara, hunting plays an important part in their lives. Another distinctive feature is the architecture of their simple homes, which are round. The Chipaya surround their villages with mud-built, whitewashed cones, in which offerings are placed to keep evil spirits away.

The Chipaya have accepted some ideas from the outside world, particularly in dress. The men now wear the tight-fitting woolen hats of the Aymara to protect themselves from the cold. They have started to wear simple rubber shoes cut from old car tires.

The Roman Catholic religion has been introduced to the Chipaya but has not replaced traditional beliefs.

THE INDIGENOUS LOWLANDERS

In isolated regions of the lowland plains, particularly in the tropical forests, there are still ethnic groups living traditional lifestyles, isolated from the outside world. These include the Guaraní, Guarayo, and Chiquitano.

Indigenous lowlanders have little in common with the rest of Bolivia. They do not speak the same language, share the same culture, or even look the same. In appearance they tend to be short, dark-skinned people with hair resembling that of peoples of African origin.

Their lifestyles are very simple. They might practice some slash-and-burn farming but generally survive on what the jungle or harsh scrubland provides for them. Technology is limited to a few simple tools and weapons. Houses are usually temporary constructions, and some of the smaller groups do not build homes at all.

Generally the indigenous peoples who lived along the rivers enjoyed the most favorable environment and developed the more advanced cultures, including complex and impressive canal systems for irrigating crops and for transportation. It was also these people who had the first contact with the Europeans, and therefore their culture has undergone the most drastic change. Many indigenous groups have abandoned their old ways of life and found work in the river settlements or rubber plantations.

The Bolivian government once offered free land to families willing to move from the crowded Altiplano to the lowlands. Thus now even the most remote peoples, who had previously managed to retain their isolated lifestyles, are finding themselves threatened as new roads are cut through the forest.

THE SPANISH

A significant number of people in Bolivia claim to be directly descended from the early Spanish colonists. Some refer to themselves as *blancos* (BLAN-kohs), meaning whites. Among these, the ones from the most conservative of prominent families refer to themselves as *la gente decente* (la HAIN-tay day-SAIN-tay), meaning "the decent people," or *la gente buena* (la HAIN-tay BWAY-nah), meaning "the good people."

It is hard to estimate how many people fall into this exact category because there has been much intermingling of the races. After four centuries, many of those who claim to be 100 percent Spanish could probably find indigenous or other blood somewhere in their family history. In the past this group was remarkably homogeneous and fiercely protective of their Spanish heritage. As a result there is a distinct group who are light-skinned and indistinguishable in appearance from people who have never left Spain.

The old-fashioned concept of "being Spanish" is made up of a combination of factors, of which purity of blood is just one. Other characteristics of being Spanish include a sense of aristocracy, a code of moral behavior, a high level of education, fluency in Spanish, European attitudes toward work, and pride in the Spanish heritage.

Although numerically small, the people of this group still have considerable influence in economics and politics. Their lifestyle generally includes all the modern luxuries. With servants and large mansions or apartments, many enjoy a higher standard of living than most North Americans. However, many Bolivians of Spanish descent have come to terms with the fact that they live in a country of cultural diversity, and give credit to Bolivia's indigenous heritage.

THE MESTIZOS

The mestizos are people of mixed Spanish and indigenous blood. They are traditionally far more likely to speak and write Spanish than the indigenous population and therefore have found it easier to become part of mainstream Bolivian society.

Many people of mixed blood still make their living from selling handicrafts, trading, and running small businesses. Since 1952 many mestizos have taken advantage of better educational opportunities, and now people of mixed blood are well established in all the major professions. Indeed they have the reputation of being shrewd at business, and there are countless legends of the wealth of the mestizos. Other Bolivians believe that even the scruffy-looking mechanic who fixes their car probably has numerous irons in the fire and a fortune in the bank.

In modern Bolivian society a few successful mestizos have even broken through Bolivia's strong class divide and become accepted into blanco society. At the same time mestizo people often retain a respect for their traditions and background. The mestizo and indigenous labels probably reflect cultural customs more than racial composition.

THE AFRO-BOLIVIANS

In the sixteenth century the Spanish brought slaves from Africa to work in the mines. The Africans were unable to adjust to the cold Altiplano climate and were resettled in the Yungas, where they worked as farmers. Up until the 1952 revolution their descendants were still working under near-slavery conditions. People today can remember being made to work in the fields when they were only six or seven years old and being whipped if they did not work hard enough.

Today there are an estimated twenty-five thousand descendants of former slaves living in Bolivia, but such estimates greatly vary from one researcher to another. They speak Spanish with a sprinkling of African words, and those around La Paz are quite likely to speak Aymara as well. Some of the women have even adopted the Aymara habit of wearing bowler hats.

Afro Bolivian men from the Yungas region perform during a 2010 carnival parade in La Paz.

Bolivians of African origin are still subject to subtle racism, with few of them attending college or holding influential positions. They have been able to make more of an impact in sports and music, and one of the few legacies of their African background is *saya* (SIE-ah) music. Consisting of chants, dancing, and rhythmic drum beats, this African sound has been passed down from generation to generation. It has even crossed over into Bolivian mainstream culture. Saya rhythms and chants are often used by fans at soccer matches.

NEW ARRIVALS

Over the years Bolivia, with its great untapped potential, has attracted various waves of immigrants seeking a better life. The arrival of new groups has often resulted from upheavals in another part of the world. The persecution of Jews before and during World War II led to a number of Polish and German immigrants going to Bolivia. They tended to settle in La Paz and Cochabamba, although many later moved on to Peru, Argentina, or Israel.

Post-World War II poverty in Japan resulted in a group of Okinawan farmers emigrating to the department of Santa Cruz. The new arrivals had to carve their homesteads out of the rain forest. At first life was very hard. The nearest town was two days away by horse, floods destroyed their first crops, and people died from the unhealthy forest climate.

Since then the community has prospered, and today their small towns are home to nearly three thousand Japanese nationals and some eleven thousand people of Japanese background. The community has hospitals built with Japanese government aid, and the city of Santa Cruz is now just a few hours away on a good road.

Japanese immigrants introduced some new agricultural ideas to Bolivia, particularly rice growing and poultry farming. Today this small area produces half of Bolivia's poultry and eggs and enough rice to have a surplus for export.

The Okinawans still maintain their Japanese culture and language, and many of the children are sent to Japan for their university education.

INTERNET LINKS

news.bbc.co.uk/2/hi/americas/7958783.stm

"Hidden Kingdom of the Afro-Bolivians" explores the lives of black Bolivians in the Yungas.

www.cocha-banner.org/issues/2013/may/okinawa

"Another Okinawa is in Bolivia, Far from Japan" looks at the Japanese community in Bolivia.

www.everyculture.com/wc/Afghanistan-to-Bosnia-Herzegovina/Aymara.html

This site provides an overview of the Aymara people and their lifestyle.

www.theguardian.com/world/2009/apr/24/andes-tribe-threat-bolivia-climate-change

This article discusses the risk of extinction of the Chipaya people.

LIFESTYLE

A llama herd is identified by the tags in the animals' ears.

7

LIFE IN THE RURAL AREAS of Bolivia has not changed much since Incan times. This is particularly true on the Altiplano, the heartland of the country. Making a living in this harsh environment requires using all the resources available. The economy still centers on livestock. Bolivia has the largest number of llamas in the world. Rural families use them for transport, meat, manure for fertilizer and fuel, and wool.

There is not much plant variety on the Altiplano, and virtually everything that grows is put to use. Thola and *yareta* are used for fuel, ichu is the main food for the llamas, and eucalyptus trees provide fuel and wood for building houses and making furniture.

One of the most useful plants is the totora reed, which grows around Lake Titicaca. These reeds can be dried for fuel, fed to the livestock, or made into small boats. The boats are mainly used for fishing, and they last less than a year before the reeds start to rot and the boat has to be replaced. Many people now have boats made from wood or fiberglass, and reed boatbuilding is becoming a dying art.

Llamas might look like harmless and cuddly animals, but they have nasty tempers and sometimes bite and spit at people who get too close.

Children sit on the street waiting for their parents in Colcha, Bolivia.

URBAN POOR

The 1952 revolution gave farmers the land they worked, but usually they have no ownership papers for the property. As such, their land cannot be sold. This means that farmers have to divide their land among their sons, so for each generation the plots of land get smaller and the people poorer. As a result, many indigenous farmers leave to seek work in the cities. The new arrivals stay with relations in the poorer neighborhoods, where living conditions are often basic, with little sanitation or heating.

Many people in low-income groups work in factories or mines. The women become street vendors, selling fruit, vegetables, or weavings, or even factory-made items ranging from plastic toys to computerized items.

Life for children of the poorest Bolivians in urban communities is worse than in rural areas, and young children often spend their days sitting on the street corner while their mothers work. Some homeless and orphaned children sleep on the street and work as shoeshine boys or as *voceadores* (voh-say-ah-DOR-ays). Voceadores work on the buses, shouting out stops and collecting fares. Increasingly, shelters are available for these children, sponsored by nongovernmental organizations.

HEALTH CARE

Health is a major issue in Bolivia. The nation has only a small budget for health care. Good medical schools produce doctors that many Bolivians cannot afford. A two-tiered system provides modern health care for the wealthy and middle class, while an underfunded public health system makes do with doctors earning working-class salaries. With little investment in rural areas, urban medical care is far superior to rural clinics. Rural Bolivians often turn to folk remedies. On the positive side, more children are now being vaccinated and more pregnant women are getting prenatal care and having skilled health practitioners attend their births.

COCA: A PART OF LIFE, AND ALSO COLA

To most indigenous highlanders, the coca leaf is more than a luxury; it is an essential commodity of life, and survival would be hard without it. The leaves are a mild narcotic and chewing them helps to numb cold, pain, and hunger. Coca leaves are made into tea and are also used medically. A cup of coca tea is a mild stimulant on par with a cup of coffee, and is said to help with altitude sickness.

According to legend, the indigenous people once tried to burn a clearing to build their homes, but the fire got out of hand and burned down part of the forest. This made the gods angry, and they sent down a thunderstorm to put out the fire. By the time the storm was over, only one tough little plant, the coca, had survived. The people chewed its leaves and found it gave them nourishment and helped them forget the hardship they had brought upon themselves.

Much of the coca grown in Bolivia is just for the domestic market, as it is illegal in many other countries, which limits its export potential. The Morales administration is trying to market alternative coca-based products, such as Coca Colla, a soft drink similar to Coca-Cola. (Coca-Cola, developed in 1886, used cocaine in its formula until 1903. Today the manufacturer still uses a cocaine-free coca leaf extract for flavor, which it obtains from coca plants brought legally into the United States from Peru and Bolivia under a special exception to the federal coca ban.) Export sales of Bolivia's Coca Colla will remain limited, however, unless international drug laws change.

ALTITUDE SICKNESS

In the high altitude of the Altiplano (12,000 feet or 3,660 m), oxygen density is lower than most visitors are used to. The first thing noticed is that a newcomer starts breathing heavily after even light exercise, such as walking upstairs. This delivers more oxygen but also puts more carbon dioxide in the blood. The victim may experience loss of appetite, feel tired, get headaches, or find thinking to be muddled.

This altitude sickness is known locally as sorojchi *(so-ROH-shay). After a couple of days these symptoms fade. People not born at high altitude will never fully adjust, as sports teams coming to play in La Paz quickly discover. Even the local people respect the altitude they live at and walk slowly. Bolivians who are not used to daily hard work also breathe heavily if they suddenly have to exert themselves.*

Nevertheless, poor hygiene and a lack of sanitation in rural areas result in frequent dysentery and worm infections. In the lowlands malaria is a constant danger. The government has put most of its limited resources into combating malaria and dysentery, though other diseases are receiving increasing attention. One of these is Chagas's disease, thought to have infected more than a million Bolivians. This disease is caused by a bug that lives in cracked walls and roofs of poorly constructed homes. At night it bites people while they sleep and sucks their blood. The feces of the insect contains a parasite that can enter the victim's body if the bite is scratched. The parasite then works itself slowly into the bloodstream. There might be some immediate signs, such as fever or swelling, but these pass. The parasite, however, remains in the blood, and years later it attacks the heart and digestive system, resulting in what appears to be sudden death.

PADRINOS

A woman in La Paz carries her baby in a traditional, woven sling.

Padrinos (pah-DREE-nohs), or godparents, play a central role for many Bolivians. To be selected as a godparent is a great honor. Rich families use the padrino system to build ties with people of equal status. Poor people might ask someone of higher status, perhaps a boss at work, to be their child's padrino. A padrino who owns a factory could not refuse to give his godchild a job, nor could he see him or her miss school because of poverty. In rural areas it is traditional for landowners, merchants, or politicians to accept many padrino commitments. This cements their position in society.

CHILDHOOD AND GROWING UP

The first years of childhood for many Bolivian children from low-income families are spent either strapped onto their mother's back or crawling around the ground playing while she works.

A hair-cutting ceremony takes place at around two years of age, which is when many children are weaned. The child's hair is braided into lots of tiny pigtails, each tied with a ribbon. The first of these locks is cut by the *padrinos*. Other relations then take turns to cut a small piece of hair according to their age and rank in the family. Each person presents the child with a gift of money, which is pinned onto the child's clothes. In rural society this money is used to buy animals. People say that crops may die, but livestock is capital for life. Herds of llamas or sheep are often tagged on the ear in different colors to mark which of the children in the family they belong to.

At eighteen boys are supposed to do a year's service in the army. Middle-class and wealthy boys often do alternative services, while some with great influence receive their military ID without serving at all. Poorer Bolivians use the military for learning skills. When they return, they are considered to have become men, and their safe return is celebrated with a large party.

HEALTH INDICATORS AND WHAT THEY MEAN

Various international organizations, including the World Health Organization (WHO) and the United Nations Children's Fund (UNICEF), compile health data for all countries. These statistics are used as a measure of a population's overall health. Two important indicators are life expectancy and infant mortality. These numbers can be used to compare health situations between countries as well as to see a country's progress (or lack of) over time. In general, Bolivia's health indicators reflect significant improvement in recent years, but remain quite poor nonetheless. Additionally, some health researchers believe Bolivia's health indicators to be out-of-date or incomplete, which of course complicates their analysis.

Life expectancy *"Life expectancy at birth" compares the average number of years a group of people born in the same year can expect to live, if mortality rates remain constant in the future. (Of course, mortality rates may well change in the future, due to medical advances, for example, but that possibility cannot be taken into account in advance, and therefore does not figure in determining life expectancy.) Life expectancy at birth is also a measure of overall quality of life in a country. Nations with longer life expectancy figures are places with higher standards of living.*

On average, a Bolivian boy born in 2015 can expect to live to age 68.8; a girl can expect to live to 71.7. In the United States, for comparison, the 2015 averages were 75 years for men and 81 for women.

Infant mortality *Infant mortality is defined as the death of an infant before his or her first birthday. It is expressed as the number of infant deaths per one thousand live births in a given place. Factors influencing infant mortality include the underlying health of the mother, public health practices, socioeconomic conditions, and availability and use of appropriate health care for infants and pregnant women.*

In Bolivia, the infant mortality in 2015 was 37.49 deaths per 1,000 live births. This compares with 9.69 out of 1,000 in neighboring Argentina, 5.87 in the United States, and 2.08 in Japan. Although Bolivia's infant mortality rate has dropped significantly—in 1980, it was 111 deaths per 1,000 live births—it remains the highest in South America.

EDUCATION

Children listen to their teacher in the elementary school in San Pablo village in the Isiboro Secure National Park and Indigenous Territory known as TIPNIS.

Education in Bolivia is free, universal, and technically compulsory. However, children in rural communities are also expected to do their share of the work on the farm, so many children drop out of school before finishing their elementary education. Urban child laborers also often miss school for economic reasons, and enforcement of compulsory education becomes difficult in such cases.

There are also cultural reasons for school dropouts. Classes are conducted in Spanish, which many indigenous children find difficult to understand. However, much progress has been made. In the 1990s bilingual education was incorporated in an increasing number of rural schools. According to official statistics, Bolivia has reached 95 percent of primary school attendance, but these statistics do not take the dropout rate into consideration.

Middle school lasts three years and high school, which is not compulsory, lasts four years. Most secondary schools are located in towns and cities, so it is very difficult for rural children to attend. Some families arrange for sons to go and live in a town with another family. That host family virtually owns the boy, who must work for them when he comes back from school. It is a very hard system but does allow a few boys from rural backgrounds to graduate. Most rural families will not permit their daughters to live away from home, which denies them the chance of a secondary education.

There has been much progress with literacy over the years, as now about 87 percent of the population can read, though this varies widely between different social classes as well as between men and women. The literacy rate is 93 percent for men and 82 percent for women.

The primary obstacle in Bolivian education concerns the huge gap in quality of education and class size between well-financed private schools and

An indigenous bride and groom are congratulated by friends and family in La Paz.

an overextended public system, in which grossly underpaid teachers cope with large class sizes and poor facilities. Until this two-tiered system is reformed, the lack of equal access to education will inhibit Bolivia's economic and social progress.

WEDDINGS

In the countryside it is common for people to live together, usually in the man's family house, before marrying. Generally after a festival, a man will persuade a woman to move in with him. This is called "stealing the girl." In the days that follow, the two families meet and negotiate the union, and then exchange gifts. The couple might stay together for years and have children before they have saved enough for a wedding with a priest and a celebration with their family and neighbors.

In urban areas Aymara, Quechua, and mestizo weddings are great occasions. Saturday is the traditional day to get married. After the service the couple stands on the church steps and the guests take turns offering congratulations. The bride and groom then climb into a taxi that has been specially rented and decorated for the occasion. The best man jumps into the front seat and the parents into the back until there are six or seven people inside, not including the driver. The other guests climb into a waiting bus, and the wedding party reassembles at a local hall for a celebration.

ROLE OF WOMEN

The rights of women are well protected by Bolivian law, but cultural and social traditions continue to hold women back.

Women do not always benefit from the laws that are there to protect them. For example, Bolivian women are entitled to three months' maternity leave. However, many women in low-paying jobs are unaware of this or afraid of losing their jobs if they take the time off.

From childhood, indigenous girls are brought up to be submissive and conservative, and although women make major contributions to the economy, they generally remain subordinate to their fathers and husbands. As a result they rarely get the chance to participate in the village meetings where decisions are made or to benefit from training programs. If they are widowed, it can be difficult for them to run the farm on their own because officials are sometimes reluctant to give them the important agricultural loans for seeds and equipment.

Unemployment is another factor that blocks female emancipation. Since it is difficult for them to find a job, women have to live with their parents until they get married as they depend on their financial support.

Women are often subjected to domestic violence. In the countryside much of this goes unreported, but in the cities it has become a far greater issue and has generated much social awareness.

In middle-class society women have previously remained largely economically inactive. This is changing rapidly, and more and more Bolivian women are moving into high-profile leadership roles.

TRADITIONAL DRESS

The traditional indigenous dress of homemade trousers and poncho is now seldom worn by men on the Altiplano; they are far more likely to wear factory-made trousers, jackets, and shirts. Traditional hats are even being replaced by baseball caps, although this fashion is popular so far only among boys and young men. For many people, *chullas* (CHOO-lahs)—woolen caps with ear flaps—remain popular, if only because they are so practical in the cold weather. The handknit chullas are exported to Europe.

Traditional dress is still widely worn by indigenous women. Aymara women are reasonably uniform in their attire, but the Quechua show more variation, particularly in hats. They wear an apron over a long skirt with many underskirts. This makes the outer skirt stick out like a hoopskirt and keeps the women warm. They are worn with an embroidered blouse, a cardigan, and a shawl called a *manta* (MAHN-tah). A vital part of the outfit is the *quepi* (k epi). These colorful rectangles can be folded to make a pouch at the back

HOUSEWIFE, MOTHER, ACTIVIST

Domitila Barrios de Chúngara (1937–2012) devoted much of her life to the struggle for economic and social justice for Bolivian miners, as well as the well-being of women in her country. Born in the mining community of Siglo XX, Chúngara grew up in extreme poverty and married a miner. In 1963 she joined the Housewives' Committee of Siglo XX, a women's group that demanded better living and working conditions for their families and their miner husbands. As one of the leaders of the committee, Chúngara participated in several hunger strikes. Once, when she was pregnant, she was jailed and tortured, and gave birth to a stillborn alone in her cell.

She became famous after publishing her autobiography Si Me Permiten Hablar *(*Let Me Speak*) with Moema Viezzer in 1978. The testimony, a first-person account of human rights abuses and living under social oppression, informed the world about the conditions in Bolivian mining towns during the 1970s. In it, she recounts the hardship and abuse that were part of everyday life. She also describes the exploitation not only by the mine owners but also by the patriarchal system in Bolivia. In 2005, she was nominated for the Nobel Peace Prize as part of the initiative "1000 Women for Peace." When Chúngara died in 2012, President Evo Morales declared three days of national mourning and awarded her the posthumous Condor of the Andes honor, the highest distinction the state can confer on a Bolivian citizen.*

to carry shopping or babies. Home-woven cloth is now giving way to brightly colored factory-made material.

Women generally wear their hair in one long braid down the back. The final touch is a hat, which is very important on the Altiplano because it gives protection from the strong winds and unfiltered sun. Across Bolivia there is a wide range of headwear, but the favorite for Aymara women is the bowler hat, known locally as the *bombín* (bohm-BEEN). The bowler hat may have been introduced to Bolivia by British railway workers, although why Aymara women rather than men started wearing them is a mystery.

Another story, probably only a legend, tells that a shipment of bowlers was sent to Bolivia by mistake and the owner sold them to the Aymara women by promising the hats would bring them fertility. For many years the Borsalino factory in Italy made hats almost entirely for the Bolivian market, although today they are produced locally.

Certain public figures proudly wear the typical *pollera* (po-YER-ah) skirt and its accessories. However, many young women are shedding the traditional dress in exchange for contemporary styles as part of western Bolivian social developments.

Bolivian women wear traditional bombín hats and pollera skirts and shawls in La Paz.

INTERNET LINKS

www.theguardian.com/world/2015/apr/22/bolivia-indigenous-women-fashion-clothing
Aymara women's fashions are showcased in this article.

nacla.org/blog/2012/3/15/remembering-domitila-making-bolivian-history
This article gives a good overview of Domitila Chúngara's life's work.

www.timeforkids.com/destination/bolivia/day-in-life
This page offers a brief "day in the life" of a twelve-year-old Bolivian boy.

magazine.worldvision.org/stories/photos-small-town-life-in-bolivia
This site presents some beautiful photos of everyday life in two rural Bolivian towns.

RELIGION

The Metropolitan Cathedral of Sucre is one of the city's landmark buildings.

8

LIKE MOST OF SOUTH AMERICA, Bolivia is predominantly Roman Catholic. Until recently, Catholicism was the official state religion, but the country's 2009 constitution established Bolivia as a secular nation. That same constitution also mandates freedom of religion, and on that score, Bolivia has a good record of tolerance.

Roman Catholicism first came to the Americas along with the Spanish conquest. Today some 76.8 percent of the population is classified as Catholic, but the number used to be much higher. However, in many places, Catholicism is mixed with indigenous beliefs, which still have a strong hold in the indigenous communities. Bolivian people say that they have one foot in the church and one foot in tradition.

The old Catholic churches are important landmarks, and the squares in front of them form meeting places and trading centers. In the cities, Bolivian churches are generally active and lively places, with people continually coming and going.

About 8 percent of the population is Protestant, and another 8 percent is Evangelical or Pentecostal. The Protestant faiths are gaining some ground in indigenous communities and in the cities.

Construction of the *Catedral Metropolitana*, or Metropolitan Cathedral of Sucre, began in 1552, but was not completed until 1712. During those 260 years, various architectural styles were introduced, and the cathedral therefore exhibits Renaissance, baroque, and mestizo baroque design features. Today, the white cathedral is one of Bolivia's most important churches.

THE INCAN RELIGION

Before the Spanish arrived, the Incas had their own religion. They believed in many different gods, built temples to honor them, and trained priests to oversee the worship. There is a great deal we don't know about the Incan religion, but it seems to have been a combination of nature worship, theological notions, animistic beliefs, and magic.

The supreme god in the Incan religion was Inti, the sun god. The emperor was regarded as the son of Inti, so that worship of Inti was tied in with worshipping the emperor. Inti's wife was Mamaquilla, the moon goddess. Pachamama ruled over the earth, Mama Cocha was the mother of the sea, and Illapa was the god of thunder and rain.

The earth was created by Viracocha, who first made giants, then, when he was unhappy with them, turned them into stone. He then came out of Lake Titicaca to create a new race, humans. Gradually, Viracocha appears to have become more important than Inti. Various historians have tried to guess the reasons for this development, but no one really knows.

A carved detail from the Gate of the Sun at the Tiwanaku archaeological site portrays the Incan god Viracocha.

The agricultural seasons were particularly important to the Incas, and great religious festivals were held at all the important stages of the farming season. People were expected to provide food and labor for the gods, and sacrifices of animals were made. Human sacrifices also took place, particularly at times of major uncertainty and upheaval, but this offering was a rare event and conducted only in the main temples.

THE OLD GODS SURVIVE

The old gods, who date to pre-Spanish (also called pre-Columbian) times, are still part of the culture of many Bolivians. People believe in these beings as gods, as superstition, or simply as part of their folklore that they wish to keep alive—or some combination of the three.

There is certainly a serious respect for Pachamama, the Incan Earth mother, which Quechua society associates with the Virgin Mary. Pachamama protects people, animals, and plants but can also be cruel and vengeful. Pachamama presides over all major events, such as marriages or giving birth, but she must also be considered when it comes to more mundane actions, such as chewing the first coca of the day.

Pachamama has the first right to all things, and whenever people start drinking alcohol, a little liquid is poured on the ground for her. Indigenous people carefully place a little chewed coca on the road as an offering before undertaking a journey. She is also honored when the first furrows are dug and at the completion of a new building.

Ekeko, which means "dwarf" in Aymara, is a pleasant little household god who retains a role in Bolivian daily life. Figurines of Ekeko portray him as a round-faced, grinning little figure laden with kitchen items. He is responsible for finding wives and husbands, for endowing good luck in business, and for providing homes. He is particularly revered in mestizo culture.

INFLUENCE OF THE JESUITS

For many years the government in the high plateau had little interest in the lowlands. Instead this area was developed by Jesuit priests, who came across the border from Paraguay. They set up around thirty communities throughout the region, each with a few priests to run them and a contingent of soldiers for protection.

The Jesuits were quite zealous in imposing their type of Catholicism on the indigenous population, and in doing so they destroyed much of the culture that had once existed in this region. In its place they introduced Spanish culture, and this still shows in the local music, which is quite different from anywhere else in Bolivia. However, when native people under Jesuit tutelage created works of art, they superimposed indigenous motifs onto the Spanish baroque style.

The Jesuit communities were well run and prosperous. The priests grew cotton, sugarcane, corn, yucca, rice, and many other fruits and vegetables. They also brought in cattle and horses. Trade grew between the lowlands and the highlands. Sugarcane, other crops, and finished works of art were exchanged for silver. The missions and their armed soldiers also protected the local people from Brazilian slave traders.

For many years the area was virtually an autonomous religious state, forming a buffer zone between the Spanish and Portuguese in South America. Eventually the Jesuits became too powerful, and the Spanish kings started to become suspicious of their activities and jealous of their wealth. Thus, in 1767 all Jesuit priests were expelled from the continent.

MIRACLES AND PILGRIMAGES

Legend has it that in the small village of Quillacollo in 1770, the youngest daughter of a poor family had the task of looking after the sheep. One day, while out in the fields, she met a beautiful woman carrying a little baby. The young girl and the woman met many times, and the daughter so enjoyed their talks that she often returned home late.

Her family did not believe her story, so one day they followed her. Seeing her parents the daughter cried out "*Ork' hopiña*," which in the Quechua language means "She is already on the mountain." With this cry the woman and baby disappeared before the eyes of the startled parents. The news spread around the village, and the people who rushed to the spot found a small image of the Virgin Mary. Today that image can be found in the village church, and every year on August 15, it is paraded around the village.

There is an important pilgrimage to Copacabana each year. The town is overlooked by a tall, steep hill called the Cerro Calvario, which has been marked out with the Stations of the Cross. At dusk on Good Friday, there is a candlelight procession from the cathedral to the top of the hill.

LIBERATION THEOLOGY

In the second half of the twentieth century, Roman Catholic priests and nuns in Latin America took an activist role in trying to improve the lives of the people they served. These clergy people believed the Gospel commanded them to liberate oppressed people from social, economic, and political repression, and created a movement that came to be called liberation theology. During some of the more oppressive dictatorships in Bolivia and elsewhere in Latin America, these Church people spoke up powerfully for human rights.

In 1980, Archbishop Jorge Manrique of La Paz opened an office to help political prisoners, while the Catholic newspaper *Presencia* and the Jesuit Radio Fides were attacked by government paramilitaries and temporarily shut down because of their outspoken journalism. At the time, Church officials in the Vatican did not endorse this movement, but Pope Francis, who began his papacy in 2013, appears more supportive.

CHA'LLA

A *cha'lla* (CHAH-ya) is a ritual blessing. It might be a Catholic event, a ceremony drawn from indigenous religion, or as is often the case, a combination of the two. It is conducted by a a Catholic priest or a *yatiri* (yah-TEE-ree), an Aymara traditional healer.

A cha'lla ceremony is performed whenever a new building is started or completed, for otherwise there will never be peace in that building. The ceremony takes place on a Saturday. The owner of the building and the workers prepare an offering, called a *cucho* (KOO-choh), consisting of a wax man, grains of incense, aromatic herbs, a few leaves of coca, cotton still on the branch, tin figures of humans and animals, and household objects, all sprinkled with an alcoholic drink.

One of the workers presides over the ceremony if a yatiri or a priest is not available. He is left alone with the cucho, which he burns. He watches the way the smoke rises to be sure all the evil spirits have left. He also asks Pachamama for her blessing. When the others return, the ashes from the offerings and any chewed coca are placed in a sack and buried in the foundations. From then on the cucho is the invisible guardian of the building.

WITCHCRAFT AND WISDOM

The yatiri is the local shaman who can be hired to help with life's problems. A yatiri may burn incense, sing chants, and make an offering to Pachamama

POPE FRANCIS IN BOLIVIA

In July 2015, Pope Francis traveled to Bolivia as part of his visit to South America. Francis himself, the former Jorge Mario Bergoglio, is Argentine and the first pope from the Americas, and he was well received. He used the opportunity to address issues that hit home with his audience. Francis had already established his position that the Church must be a refuge and advocate for the poor and dispossessed. In Bolivia, however, he went further. Speaking in Santa Cruz, the pope apologized for the Roman Catholic Church's oppression of Latin America during the colonial era.

"I say this to you with regret: Many grave sins were committed against the native people of America in the name of God," Francis said, adding, "I humbly ask forgiveness, not only for the offense of the church herself, but also for crimes committed against the native peoples during the so-called conquest of America."

The pope's visit came at a time when Roman Catholicism in Bolivia is weakening. More and more people have stopped practicing, and some have converted to Evangelical faiths. Some 60 percent of Protestants in Bolivia say they were raised Catholic. In addition, under the administration of Evo Morales, the country switched from being an officially Catholic state to a secular one.

Francis did not merely apologize for the Church, however. He also praised the courage of many Latin American priests and lay Catholics who have stood up for indigenous rights, and expressed his vision of Roman Catholicism as a positive force for peace and justice.

at a sacred place on a client's behalf. If a client seeks advice on matters such as marriage or a business venture, a yatiri might conduct a fortune-telling reading of coca leaves. *Amauta* (ah-MOW-tah) are also wise men. In Incan society the amauta had to remember vast amounts of information because there were no written records. They are still respected for their wisdom.

Many people believe in harmful spirits. *Karisirus* are night phantoms who catch people out after dark or when they are sleeping. According to legend, they split their victim's stomach and extract some of the fat. In rural areas mothers call their children indoors with a warning about the karisirus to make them come home quicker.

In La Paz, the Mercado de las Brujas, or Witches' Market, caters to both locals and tourists in selling a wide selection of Andean herbs, folk remedies, figurines, and other ritualistic items, including dried llama fetuses, which are used as offerings in cha'lla ceremonies to Pachamama.

INTERNET LINKS

news.nationalgeographic.com/news/2003/05/0530_030530_witchdoctors.html
This is an article about the Witches' Market in La Paz.

www.state.gov/j/drl/rls/irf/2007/90243.htm
The US State Department's International Religious Freedom Report (2007) for Bolivia can be found here.

www.telegraph.co.uk/travel/destinations/southamerica/bolivia/729642/Bolivia-A-spell-in-a-high-place.html
This travel article focuses on witchcraft and coca in Bolivia.

w2.vatican.va/content/francesco/en/speeches/2015/july/documents/papa-francesco_20150709_bolivia-movimenti-popolari.html
The English transcript of Pope Francis's 2015 speech in Bolivia can be found on this Vatican site.

A school mural in Spanish warns children not to accept strangers as friends on Facebook.

9

The group Jaqi Aru works to encourage indigenous young people by promoting the use of the Aymara language on the internet. A group of volunteers in Bolivia is working to translate Spanish-language Facebook into the Aymara language. Facebook requires a translation of twenty-four thousand words before it will launch the site in a new language.

LANGUAGE IS POWERFUL. OFTEN IT is a reflection of political power—or lack of. When a multilingual country establishes an official language, the speakers of that language automatically accrue political and social legitimacy. Unofficial languages and those who speak them, therefore, acquire a lower status.

Ever since Spain conquered the Incas five centuries ago, Spanish has been the dominant language and *lingua franca* of Bolivia. Although the indigenous people of Bolivia spoke a variety of native tongues, the accepted notion—at least among the people in power—was that the best way to build a strong sense of nationhood was through one common language. (Of course, this idea is hardly unique to Bolivia.) To that end, schoolchildren were taught exclusively in Spanish and everyone was expected to speak Spanish. Native languages were encouraged to wither away, and many did.

In the later part of the twentieth century, indigenous groups began to question that policy. Education reform in the 1990s brought intercultural bilingual education to Bolivia. When Evo Morales, an Aymara speaker, was first elected president in 2006, he set out to correct language inequities—and by extension, social and political ones as well. Under his leadership, the new Bolivian constitution, ratified in 2009, establishes "all" indigenous languages as official, along with Spanish. Curiously, the document lists thirty-six native languages, even more than are spoken in the country, since several have become extinct. Nevertheless,

A man in La Paz reads Spanish-language newspaper headlines announcing President Morales's victory in the 2014 election.

the inclusion of these languages is a symbolic act of equality. From a practical standpoint, though, it could be a logistical nightmare to enforce. Therefore, the constitution does not require the Bolivian government to conduct its business in all thirty-seven languages. However, all departmental governments must now use one indigenous language in addition to Spanish.

Despite this accomplishment, some Bolivians do speak languages that are not deemed official. Various waves of immigrants have brought their home languages with them. In a few lowland towns, one could probably communicate just as easily in Japanese as in Spanish, and in the Santa Cruz Department, a community of some seventy thousand Mennonites speaks a German dialect.

Of the native languages, Aymara and Quechua are the most widely spoken. About 14.6 percent of Bolivians speak Aymara, and 21.1 percent speak Quechua. Spanish remains the most important language of commerce, art, broadcasting, and politics. About two-thirds of the population speaks Spanish as their first language. Although Aymara and Quechua are widespread, many indigenous people speak Spanish too.

QUECHUA AND AYMARA

Quechua and Aymara are quite similar in some ways, such as in how words are compounded. Some linguists believe they might be related. Indeed someone who does not speak either language might listen to them and think they were the same. The vocabulary, however, is very different, and Quechua and Aymara speakers cannot understand each other.

In the past, few Spanish speakers bothered to learn either of these Andean languages, preferring that the indigenous population learn Spanish. With interest increasing in indigenous culture, this situation is slowly changing.

However, even Spanish speakers who are willing to try to learn one of their nation's other official languages do not necessarily find it easy to do so. The sound of both Aymara and Quechua is very different from most European languages, and this makes them difficult for Spanish speakers to learn. (Of course, the reverse was also true for the indigenous people learning Spanish.) There are also other differences. For example, the power and force with which some sounds are delivered are an important part of the communication, as is leaving a slight pause between some sounds.

The major Bolivian media do little to cater to Aymara and Quechua speakers, although radio and television do give the news in the two indigenous languages. These programs are usually broadcast early in the morning, before the farming community starts work. One radio program even carries personal messages, uniting family members who live far apart. Enterprising Aymaras and Quechuas have created local community radio stations that serve their immediate regions.

Men listen to an indigenous radio station.

QUECHUA Quechua was the language of the Incan Empire and is still spoken by eight million indigenous people in Peru, Bolivia, Ecuador, Chile, and northwest Argentina. This makes it an important international language. Because it covers such a wide area and so many different groups, Quechua has many different dialects. Some Quechua speakers would understand each other only with difficulty.

Recently scholars have come up with the idea of writing out common rules and vocabulary to unify the language. However, Quechua is largely an oral language with little written tradition, so this idea has not gone far.

AYMARA The Aymara people retained their language despite attempts to suppress it by both the Incas and the Spanish. Today it is spoken by about 2.5 million people in Peru, Bolivia, Argentina, and Chile. It is a harsh, guttural-sounding language, with sounds coming from the back of the throat.

BEWARE OF FALSE FRIENDS

Many Spanish and English words look and sound the same. There are two reasons for this. Some words are similar because they originally came from the same Latin root. Other words have been borrowed from the other language. For example, Spanish has given the English language words such as alligator, tomato, guitar, cork, armada, *and* vanilla. *A few words have even passed from Aymara or Quechua to Spanish, and from there to English. The best example of this is* llama *from Quechua.*

Spanish also has many words that look the same as English words but have a different meaning. For example, la carpeta *might be thought to mean "the carpet," but in fact it means "folder."* Jubilación *is not the Spanish word for "jubilation," but means "retirement." Such words are called false friends and are something people have to be aware of when learning Spanish.*

Legend has it that four thousand years ago a group of wise men sat down and made up the language from scratch. The Jesuit missionary Ludovico Bertonio, who wrote the first Aymara-Spanish dictionary in 1610, described Aymara as a "genius of a language" because it is so well thought-out, with easy-to-understand linguistic rules.

Since 1984, Aymara has been used in multilingual computerized translation. Iván Guzmán de Rojas, a Bolivian mathematician, created a computer program using Aymara as the intermediary language to translate European languages.

SPANISH

Spanish is one of the Romance languages, which means it originated from Latin. A version of vulgar, or common, Latin was first brought to Spain by Roman soldiers and settlers. Over the centuries it underwent many other influences until, by the Middle Ages, a distinctive Spanish language had emerged.

When the Spanish built up their huge colonial empire, they introduced their language to regions they conquered. As a result, about 410 million people around the world now speak Spanish as a first language, and businesspeople from Cuba, Bolivia, and Spain could quite happily communicate with each other in their common language. Spanish is also one of the official languages of the United Nations.

The Spanish spoken in Bolivian highlands is slower than what is heard in Spain, and most Bolivian people do not drop syllables as much. Some of the sounds are also different. The *z* and *ci* in words such as *manzana* and *gracias* are pronounced as a *th* sound in Spain but as an *s* sound in Bolivia.

Bolivian Spanish has adopted many words from the Andean languages. Examples of Quechua words used by Spanish-speaking Bolivians include *wawa* (baby), *imilla* (girl), and *ilokalla* (boy).

A road sign picturing a llama cautions drivers to watch out for animals in the mountains.

INTERNET LINKS

www.omniglot.com
This language site gives an excellent introduction to the Aymara, Quechua, and Spanish languages, with alphabets and pronunciation guides.

www.timeforkids.com/destination/bolivia/native-lingo
Listen to a few common phrases in Aymara on this page.

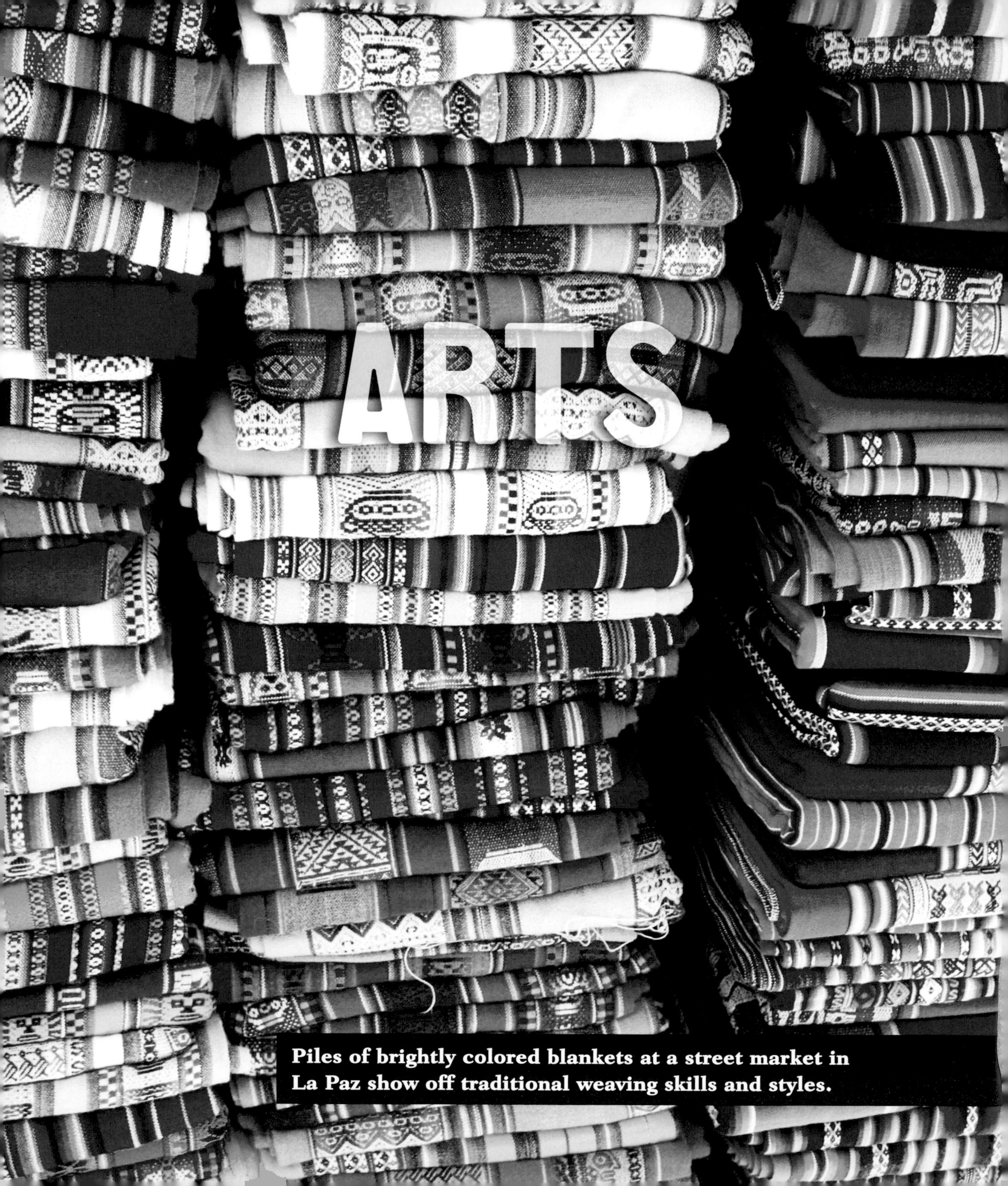

ARTS

Piles of brightly colored blankets at a street market in La Paz show off traditional weaving skills and styles.

WONDERFUL WEAVINGS

Along with llamas and women in bowler hats, some of the most iconic images associated with Bolivia are the textiles. Colorful folk weavings have been an important craft in indigenous culture since Incan times. Traditional designs differ regionally among the various groups of native peoples, according to their own customs. Although both men and women weave, it is primarily a job for women, and children begin learning as young as five years old. In many communities, women have formed cooperative weavers' organizations to make, market, and sell their wares. For Andean women, weaving is an important source of income in a region that offers little alternative. First and foremost, however, their textiles are used to make clothing, rugs, and blankets for their own families.

Typically, the weaver works at a homemade manual loom using alpaca wool. An alpaca is similar to a small llama, but has softer fleece. People also weave with llama wool, but it is coarser and less desirable than alpaca. In Tarabuco, in the central part of the country, weavers might use cotton or sheep's wool. First the fiber is spun on a small spindle into a single strand. It is then transferred to a larger spindle and spun into a two-ply yarn. After being dyed it is given a third spin. It is this third spin that gives Bolivian cloth its strength, elasticity, and hard, smooth surface.

The artisans dye the wool using natural colorants made from local plants. They usually create traditional designs using geometric patterns and animal shapes. The results are not only beautiful, but individual and full of meaningful symbolism.

10

IT IS SAID THAT IN BOLIVIA THE BEST art is not found in museums but on the streets. The country boasts a rich heritage of folk arts, particularly weaving, and many artisans sell their wares at market stalls in the cities. Bolivian weaving is considered to be of a particularly high quality, and tourists often seek out handcrafted blankets, shawls, belts, and other woolens at these markets.

In 2014, the Pujllay (rainy season) and Ayarichi (dry season) music and dances of the Yampara culture in Bolivia were named to the UNESCO list of Intangible Cultural Heritage of Humanity.

The streets are also where music and dance can be found, especially during festivals. The costumes and masks created for these fiestas are works of art unto themselves. Even many of the traditional musical instruments qualify as folk arts, as they are made the old-fashioned way, by hand. The charango, for example, a sort of small Andean lute which was probably first created in the Bolivian city of Potosi during colonial times, is still made by hand in Cochabamba and other places.

DANCE

The folk dances that are performed today are a combination of pre-Columbian dances, Spanish dances, and African dances. One of the most famous is the *cueca* (KWAY-kah), or handkerchief dance. The *cueca* can trace its roots through the Chilean cueca to the Spanish fandango.

Many celebrations would not be complete without a festive *caporales*, a traditional Andean dance with roots in Afro-Bolivian Saya, which originated in the Yungas region. Like the cueca, caporales is a legacy of the Spanish conquest. In the dance, a man depicts an old Spanish guard, or foreman, in charge of slaves in colonial times. His elaborate costume includes heeled boots adorned with large bells known as *cascabeles*, and a whip to be carried in his right hand. Some dancers carry a hat instead. The bells are supposed to signify the sound of the chains on the ankles of the slaves. Women wear bowler hats, very short flouncy dresses, and fancy heeled shoes. The dance is a march, and therefore is often included in festival parades. There is a lot of drumming, and spectators clap along.

Aymara women dance at a festival in the village of Cha'llapama on Isla del Sol in Lake Titicaca.

Another popular dance is the Diablada, or Dance of the Devils. The dance is the centerpiece of the Oruro Carnival, Bolivia's top tourist attraction. This dance also dates to colonial times and mixes indigenous elements with Spanish culture, and there are regional variations. It is a highly theatrical dance, performed with ornate costumes of devils and angels. The dance incorporates elements of Incan religious ceremonies, Aymaran miners' rituals, and Christian iconography.

These are just three of a wide variety of traditional dances, which are as different as the people and regions of Bolivia.

VISUAL ARTS

The Incas were magnificent artists, but their best work in gold and silver was melted down by the Spaniards. Modern Bolivian art started with the colonial period, and the first artwork was religious. The most renowned artist of that period was Melchor Pérez de Holguín, who was born in 1660. His religious paintings contain many strange touches. In one painting, a saint talks to an angel, while in the background an alien-looking bird attacks a frog.

Church authorities employed mestizo artists, and in the seventeenth and eighteenth centuries a mestizo baroque style developed that mixed indigenous and Spanish styles.

The fathers of contemporary Bolivian art are Cecilio Guzmán de Rojas and Arturo Borda. Guzmán studied in Madrid, returning to Bolivia in 1929. He was one of the first painters to portray indigenous subjects, and Machu Picchu in Peru was a favorite theme. He also depicted the beauty and nobility of the indigenous Andean people. His style was influenced by cubism. On the other hand, Borda covered a wide range of subjects. A favorite was Mount Illimani, which he painted from all angles and in all different kinds of light.

Women artists have had much success in Bolivia too. María Núñez del Prado created sculptures from natural materials that were heavily influenced by the indigenous cultures. María Luisa Pacheco was a student of Guzmán but spent most of her career in the United States.

An easy way to begin appreciating modern Bolivian art would be to view the historic murals of Walter Solon Romero, often found in public buildings, especially in Sucre and La Paz. Edgar Arandia and Roberto Mamani Mamani take Bolivian art on two unique but colorful paths.

TRADITIONAL MUSIC

Much of Bolivia's traditional music is based on simple instruments that boys play to pass the long hours while they are looking after the animals. As a result every village, even every street, usually has its own band.

Although the music and dance of the Altiplano are considered representative of Bolivia, in fact there is a remarkable degree of regional variation. The music of the cold, harsh Altiplano tends to be sad and mournful, but in the lowlands music is faster and more lively. Chaco music is the most distinctive and concentrates more on violin, drum, and guitar. This is largely due to the influence of Jesuit priests, who taught the indigenous peoples to play European instruments.

A HOLLYWOOD MYTH OR TRUTH?

The most famous movie to feature Bolivia is Butch Cassidy and the Sundance Kid *(1969). The Hollywood hit stars Paul Newman and Robert Redford and follows the path of two outlaws who flee from the United States to Bolivia. The movie is based on a well-known story of western folklore, but nobody is sure what is truth and what is legend.*

However, historians have hunted through old Bolivian mining records and discovered that in 1908 there indeed was a series of robberies by two North American bandits. Local people knew where the graves of the two bandits were supposed to be and led investigators to the spot. When the investigators dug, they found two skeletons. The DNA tests supposedly proved the remains were not those of Butch and Sundance, and some people believe the two made it back to the United States where they lived out their lives. However, the controversy continues to this day.

The most important recent trend is to introduce lyrics to the mournful Andean music, creating a new genre of folk songs. Folk musicians have the opportunity to play in street festivals, and the best groups might be invited to perform at a *peñas* (PAY-nyas). These are folk music shows that take place in restaurants.

Los Kjarkas is the best known of the Bolivian folk groups and plays a stylized kind of modern folk song. Other well-known groups include Savia Andina, popular for its poetic lyrics and love songs, and Wara, which has successfully combined traditional and modern music genres. Wara is also considered the best of the traditional Aymara groups.

MUSICAL INSTRUMENTS

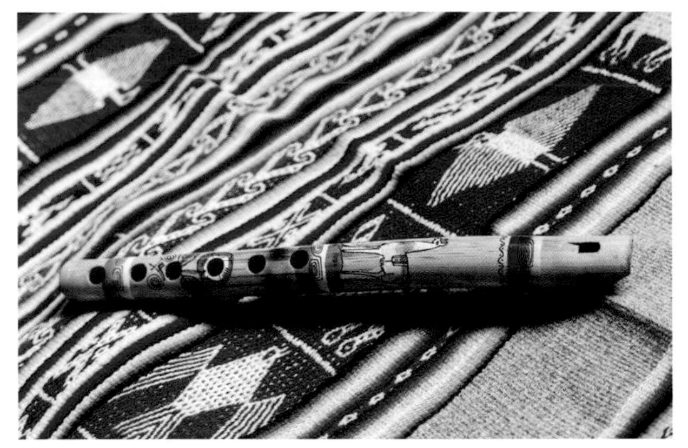

Traditional Bolivian instruments generally come in families of small, large, and medium sizes. Most typical are the simple flutes made from reed pipes, which are known as quenas *(KAY-nas), and the more complicated* zampoña *(zahm-POH-nya).*

The quena *does not have a mouthpiece, but is played by blowing into a notch in the instrument. Traditionally it was a solo instrument, but it is now often incorporated into a musical ensemble. One recognized master of the reed flute is Gilbert Fabre.*

Zampoñas, also known as panpipes, or by the Aymara name of siku *(SEE-koo), are more complicated and consist of a collection of different-sized reeds lashed together. The sound is produced by forcing air across the open end of the reeds. It is the zampoña that gives Bolivian musical troupes much of their distinctive sound.*

Shells and cow horns might also be used, and drums have also become a central part of Andes music, although many of the designs are based on Spanish military drums. String instruments include the charango *(chah-RAN-goh), a small, guitarlike instrument with a high twangy sound. The* charango *was once made from an armadillo shell, but today, for ecological reasons, it is made of wood. Unlike the guitar, it has ten strings arranged in pairs, and the best* charangos *are prized works of art. Another string instrument is the* violin chapaco, *a variation of the European violin.*

Despite a growing influence from the Western music that is carried into the remotest homes by radio, traditional Bolivian folk music remains the most popular. Using authentic instruments, American musician Paul Simon recorded a version of the Andean folk song "El Condor Pasa," which has become a classic pop song in both Europe and North America.

In Bolivia, October 11 is celebrated as the "Day of Bolivian Women." The date is the birthday of Adela Zamudio (1854–1928), a poet, feminist, and educator who is considered Bolivia's most famous poet.

INTERNET LINKS

asur.org.bo/en/textiles

This organization, which runs the Museum of Indigenous Arts in Sucre, presents information about traditional textiles.

boliviandances.blogspot.com

This site presents information, photos, and videos of many kinds of traditional Bolivian dances.

www.historynet.com/butch-cassidy

content.time.com/time/world/article/0,8599,1951085,00.html

Two interesting takes on the Butch Cassidy story are offered here. The *Time* article also discusses how the legend has benefited the Bolivian town of San Vincente.

www.ipsnews.net/2012/04/native-andean-women-weave-a-future-in-bolivia

This article describes indigenous women's weaving organizations.

www.notesonslowtravel.com/famous-traditional-dances-in-bolivia

Festive Bolivian folk costumes and dances are the subject of this entry, with excellent photos.

www.unesco.org/culture/ich/en/RL/pujllay-and-ayarichi-music-and-dances-of-the-yampara-culture-00630

This UNESCO page, featuring Yampara dances and music selected for the Intangible Cultural Heritage list, includes an excellent video.

LEISURE

Bolivia's Yasmani Duk celebrates after scoring against Paraguay during a World Cup qualifying match in 2015.

11

FOR SOME BOLIVIANS, LEISURE TIME is a foreign concept. In the San Miguel neighborhood of La Paz, for example, a woman named Sofi works at a food stall selling *tucumana*, a deep-fried meat pastry. She works seven days a week and takes only one day off a year, on Christmas. As is true in many countries, the hardworking poor like Sofi have little time for leisure.

A woman cooks at a food stall at the Mercado Central Market in Tarija, Bolivia.

Bolivia's national soccer team plays at the Estadio Hernando Siles in La Paz. At 11,932 feet (3,637 m) above sea level, it is one of the highest stadiums in the world. In 2007, FIFA, the world soccer federation, banned World Cup qualifying matches from high-altitude stadiums because their thin air is a disadvantage for visiting teams. However, after Bolivian complaints, FIFA made a special exemption for the La Paz stadium.

For those who can afford to take time off, however, holidays and weekends are a time to spend with friends and family. On special occasions such as weddings or festivals, family gatherings involve a considerable amount of singing, dancing, and feasting. At other times, such as on a quiet weekend, time together is more likely to be spent lingering over a leisurely meal with the traditional conversation hour afterward.

In cities, public parks form an important part of social life. The park is a place where children play soccer and ride their bikes. Adults sit in the sun talking, and teenage couples cuddle together on benches, oblivious to everybody around them. Generally when adults sit in the park, they seem happy enough just to pass the time in conversation, but groups of men might play cards or dice.

Many people belong to special dance clubs that devote months practicing to perform at major festivals. Members of dance teams might spend several hundred dollars on their elaborate costumes.

For indigenous women, free time is largely spent knitting or weaving. Partly this might be considered work because many of the items they make will be sold for extra income. However, the women feel a great deal of pleasure and pride from their handicraft.

CHILDREN'S GAMES

Many Bolivian children have little money to spend on toys, so they have to improvise their own games or make their own toys with what materials they can find. An old bicycle wheel will become a hoop, a pile of stones work as building blocks.

The most popular game of all is spinning tops, and small wooden tops are for sale in every market. The game is usually played by boys from the ages of seven or eight through the early teenage years. Most boys like to spin the top and then slide two fingers underneath it and try to pick it up while it is still spinning. Once the top is in their hand, they will try to drop it onto an upturned bottle cap.

Marbles, using factory-made glass marbles, is another popular game. The players each place a marble in a circle drawn in the dirt. Taking turns, they then flick a second marble into the arena. From this point on, players win any marble they hit with their marble. Although seemingly simple, the game has many additional rules that the boys playing all seem to understand.

Other common street games include clapping games, chase games, and games played with stones, where players try to throw their stones as close to a mark on the ground as possible.

In the rural areas, slingshots made from forked tree branches and old elastic strips are popular. This game allows boys to practice their skill and is useful in scaring birds off the crops.

Bolivian swimmer Sergio Villarroel competes during the VII International Open Water Swimming Tournament at Lake Titicaca in 2013.

TRADITIONAL SPORTS

Apart from soccer, which is played nearly everywhere, sports are largely enjoyed by the urban population. For the majority of Bolivians in the countryside, life is simply too hard to leave them with much energy or enthusiasm for sports.

Bolivia does have a few traditions that could be considered sports. *Tinku* (TEEN-koo), which takes place on rural highland festival days, is a bare-fisted type of boxing that starts off as a highly ritualistic dance and usually breaks down into a free-for-all in which the contestants try to knock each other down by any means possible. Fists and feet fly, and the whole event is a great favorite with crowds. Indeed, as people get more and more excited, the violence often spills over into the audience. This modern version is tame compared with earlier versions, when the boys taking part used slings to throw cacti at each other.

There is also a yearly swimming race across the narrowest part of Lake Titicaca. The distance is not particularly long, but the water is extremely cold, making it a test of endurance for the competitors. Another annual event limited to those with mythical stamina is the La Paz marathon, held at 12,000 feet (3,660 m) above sea level, with some of the most grueling uphill terrain known in the sport.

A NATION OF SOCCER LOVERS

Soccer is the national sport of Bolivia and is played everywhere, from parks to the street. Supporters show their loyalty to the best teams by placing stickers in their cars or by wearing replicas of their favorite team's shirts.

Important games are played at the national stadium in La Paz, where the home team, nicknamed *La Verde* ("The Green"), always has a great advantage because of the altitude. Bolivian players are accustomed to the thinner air (lower oxygen), whereas visiting teams can't acclimate sufficiently in just a few days. As a result, Bolivia has won many of its international games. The most notable occasion came in 1963, when the national team won the South American Championship in its own high-altitude stadium.

The team qualified for the World Cup in 1994 and Bolivia hosted the 1997 South American Championship. After that, Bolivia's team endured a long losing streak until the 2015 Copa América (formerly the South American Championship), when it defeated Ecuador 3—2.

The Bolivian Professional Football League's First Division comprises twelve clubs, with many other clubs in lower subdivisions. Traditionally the

Children play soccer in the streets of Cochabamba.

best teams are Club Bolívar and The Strongest, with the relatively new La Paz Fútbol Club doing well in third place.

Soccer is not just a game for professional players. Hundreds of men, but very few women, play soccer for recreation. The better players may belong to local teams that have team uniforms and play on full-sized fields, although they will generally be fields of mud or sand rather than grass. Less serious players join casual games in the park. These games are usually played on a concrete arena the size of a basketball court, with four or five players on each team. The games end when the first goal is scored, the winners staying to play the next opponents.

OTHER SPORTS

Bolivians play many different sports, and every four years they send a small team to the Olympic Games. However, they have yet to win an Olympic medal. In the Pan American Games, held between all nations of the Americas, Bolivia has done slightly better. At the 2015 Pan American Games in Toronto, thirty-four athletes competed for Bolivia in twelve sports, winning one silver and two bronze medals. Those results landed Bolivia in twentieth place (tied with three other nations) out of twenty-eight rankings.

Basketball is the second most popular sport, followed by volleyball, and there are nationwide league competitions for both sports.

Wealthy people are likely to try sailing or golf. La Paz has the highest golf course in the world. Because of the thin air, players find they can hit the ball longer distances than at sea level. Tennis and racquets are also popular. The latest craze with the rich Bolivians is motor sports, particularly go-carts and motorbike racing. Some of the world's toughest long-distance rally races pass through Bolivia.

Gravity-assisted cycling is another breathtaking sport, especially enjoyed by tourists. Starting in the cold mountains and wheeling downhill around scary hairpin turns, swerving away from the deep gorges, cyclists will reach the hot lowlands after six hours of fright and delight.

Bolivia's North Yungas Road, better known as "The Death Road," has become a popular though deadly destination for thrill-seeking tourists like this bike rider. About 25,000 mountain bike riders descend the 40-mile (64 km) road each year, of which some 200 to 300 die annually.

WEEKENDS

Friday night is a popular time to go out on the town. One traditional Friday night activity, mainly among some middle-class men, is known as *viernes de soltero* (VYAIR-nays day sohl-TAY-roh), or single man's Friday, when even married men pretend they are single for the night and drink and play dice or cards. Many of their wives go out with each other rather than sit at home waiting for their husbands.

Bolivians of all ages and all social classes love to dance. Sometimes they partner across age lines in family gatherings or else join peer groups or schoolmates. The excuse for such get-togethers is often a birthday or traditional celebration. Sunday afternoons are usually reserved for family gatherings and barbecues, while various cities open their downtowns as strolling areas.

In the cities there are also cultural activities such as concerts and art expositions. Some people like to get together in intellectual cafés and debate on various subjects.

MOUNTAIN MAN

The Bolivian Andes offer some of the most spectacular mountain climbing in the world. The king of Bolivian mountain climbing is Bernardo Guarachi (b. 1952), a man of native Aymara descent, who was born near the Altiplano village of Patacamaya.

Guarachi has been to the top of Illimani, the highest mountain in Bolivia, at least 192 times. One of the most memorable times was early in his career, in 1985, when a US commercial airline jet crashed into the side of the mountain, killing everyone onboard. Guarachi and two assistants were the only people capable of reaching the crash site to confirm the situation.

In 1998, Guarachi became the first Bolivian to reach the summit of Mount Everest. For that feat, he was honored with a Bolivian postage stamp the following year. His goal now is to climb the Seven Summits, the highest mountains of each of the seven continents. As of 2010, only 275 people had accomplished this top mountaineering challenge. Guarachi, who climbs with his son Eliot, had summitted four of the peaks as of 2015. Meanwhile, when he isn't climbing for his own sake, he runs Andes Expediciones, an adventure travel and mountain climbing company.

INTERNET LINKS

andesexpediciones.com/en/bernardo-guarachi
The home site of Andes Expediciones has news stories and photos of Bernardo Guarachi.

www.fifa.com/associations/association=bol
This is the Bolivia page of the FIFA site.

FESTIVALS

A car is ready for its blessing in front of the cathedral in Copacabana in August 2014.

12

BOLIVIAN FESTIVALS ARE SOME of the most colorful in the world. Bolivians are usually happy to celebrate, whatever the occasion, and festivals quickly turn into lively parties with street parades, dance, music, fireworks, craft sales, games, piñatas, feasting, and drinking. There are ancient festivals that date to Incan times and religious celebrations that are the legacy of centuries of Spanish rule. At fiesta time, the two cultures often become interwoven, with older Incan ceremonies being incorporated into modern religious celebrations.

Some fiestas are celebrated throughout the country, and others are regional. Each department has its own public holiday, and most towns and villages have a festival for their special patron saint. There are other events that take place several times a year or even weekly. Fiestas are an important part of religious life and are major social occasions that bind communities together. Influential individuals who sponsor the fiestas often do so to secure their own position in society and build on their power and prestige.

In the town of Copacabana, Bolivia, people gather on the shores of Lake Titicaca for a daily car blessing ceremony. In front of the Basilica of Our Lady of Copacabana, flower-bedecked cars line up to await a priest, who sprinkles holy water on the vehicles. After the blessing, the car's owner will often pop a bottle of champagne, beer, or even cola, and spray it over the car before driving off.

A woman in La Paz sells figures of Ekeko, the Aymara god of abundance, during the Alasitas Festival.

NEW YEAR'S

The new year is celebrated with one great party. Generally families gather at one house and see the new year in together. After midnight the younger people might go to a nightclub while the older family members continue the party at home.

On these occasions the host family provides food, but it is common for everyone to pay something toward the cost. A pork stew called *fricasé* (FREE-kah-say) is served very early in the morning. After that people drift home to sleep.

An increasingly common alternative for wealthy people is to attend an organized New Year's celebration at their sports or social club.

ALASITAS FESTIVAL

Alasitas (ah-lah-SEE-tahs), or the "Festival of Abundance," is an Aymara festival that takes place in La Paz and around Lake Titicaca. It is held on different dates in different towns, but in the capital it takes place on January 24. Originally Alasitas was held to ensure a good crop and was staged in September, which is the Bolivian spring. The Spanish moved the festival to January.

The festival centers on Ekeko, the god of the household and possessions. On the festival day, street stalls sell models of Ekeko and tiny accessories that people can buy for him. These represent all the things people wish to receive themselves.

It is thought to bring good luck to buy these items at exactly noon, which means there is a terrible rush with everybody pushing and shoving. It is also considered to be luckier still to have the items given to you by a friend than to buy them yourself.

ORURO FESTIVAL

The largest carnivals are generally those staged in February and March, in the weeks leading up to Lent. All major Bolivian towns stage weeklong festivals at this time, but the largest and most famous takes place in the high-altitude mining town of Oruro. It's one of Bolivia's greatest tourist attractions.

The festival is based on local folklore. Legend tells that the Virgin of Candelaria took pity on a thief who had been mortally wounded in a robbery and helped him home so he could die in his own village. The next morning the local people found his body draped over a statue of the Virgin.

The grand parade takes part on the opening day of the festival. Cars and trucks decorated with jewelry, coins, and silver lead the procession. Next

Fantastical costumes make the Oruro carnival a colorful occasion.

Participants dress in purple at a Good Friday procession in La Paz.

come the dance troupes led by the Archangel Michael, dressed in sky blue and carrying his sword and shield. He is followed by people dressed as bears, condors, and devils. The devil figures wear the biggest masks of all. These are carved with horns and serpents, and sometimes even have bulging flashing lights for eyes. After that there are marchers dressed as Incas, Kallawaya medicine men, dancers with headdresses of tropical feathers, conquistadores, and miners carrying gifts for El Tío (the devil).

The parade finishes at the stadium with the folk dance, La Diablada ("Dance of the Devils"). Supay (SOO-pay), an evil spirit believed to live in the center of the Earth, fights Saint Michael in a ritual dance, in which the forces of good triumph over evil.

In 2001, UNESCO (the United Nations Educational, Scientific and Cultural Organization) declared the Oruro Festival one of the "Masterpieces of the Oral and Intangible Heritage of Humanity."

EASTER

Semana Santa, or Holy Week, is the week leading up to Easter Sunday. During Semana Santa, many towns and cities will hold processions of faithful and special church services. Unlike Christmas, the date for Easter is changeable, and occurs in March or April, and marks Christ's resurrection from the dead. Easter is observed throughout Bolivia as a religious holiday, although symbolic or secular elements, such as chocolate Easter bunnies, are catching on.

FIESTA DEL GRAN PODER

Fiesta del Gran Poder (el grahn poh-DAIR), or the "Festival of the Great Power," began in 1939 as a simple candlelit procession through the streets of La Paz paying homage to Señor del Gran Poder, or Jesus Christ. Since then,

El Gran Poder has grown to become today's great street parade.

Celebrated in late May or early June, the parade extends 8 miles (13 km) through the streets of La Paz, testing the stamina of the dancers and marching bands, and delighting the crowds of people, who come from all over the world. The range of costumes is magnificent and reflects every aspect of Bolivian history and mythology, including both Aymara folklore and Catholic traditions. The parade lasts around twelve hours, with partying continuing well into the night.

Lavishly dressed dancers parade in the streets of La Paz during El Gran Poder.

INTI RAYMI / FIESTA DE SAN JUAN BATISTA

The elaborate Inti Raymi, or "Festival of the Sun," is observed on the shortest day of the year, which in the Southern Hemisphere is the June solstice. This revived version of an old Incan ritual honors the god Inti and is popular in Peru. In the Bolivian Andes regions, it often incorporates festivities for San Juan Batista (St. John the Baptist), which occur at the same time. The Catholic festival of San Juan Batista coincides with the winter solstice and harvest season. People set off fireworks and light bonfires, leaping over the flames to bring good luck. The fires also represent the warmer months that lie ahead.

FIESTA DEL ESPÍRITU

The Fiesta del Espíritu is rooted in the mining traditions of Potosí. It is an occasion for the miners to make an offering to Pachamama, the Earth Mother, in the hope that she will protect them. The festival is staged on the last three Saturdays in June, and then again in August.

A nativity scene features the Holy Family wearing indigenous clothing.

In the days leading up to the festival, villagers bring llamas into town, until the streets look like one great animal market. Each mine selects one of their workers to buy a llama for their mine. The purchases take place on the morning of the festival and are followed by an hour or so of drinking and chewing coca. At midday the llamas are sacrificed. Some of the blood is caught and thrown down the mine, and later the stomach, feet, and head are buried as a further offering. After the sacrifice the men return to their drinking while the women prepare the llama meat for the feast that follows.

CHRISTMAS

In urban areas of Bolivia, Christmas is celebrated in much the same way as in Europe or the United States. Celebrations in the countryside, however, are more of an agricultural festival. Occurring at the time of the Southern Hemisphere's Summer Solstice, Christmas celebrations often incorporate elements of the Incan Festival of the Sun. At this time of year the crops have just been planted and the llamas have given birth, so life on the earth is very vulnerable. The Aymara used to make little clay models of each of their animals at this time to bring good luck, but the tradition has died out. Aymara people attend church on Christmas but do not give gifts.

Traditionally, groups of children dress in costumes and walk the streets singing *villancicos* (vee-yan-SEE-kos), or Christmas carols, and playing drums and other instruments. It's customary to give the children small gifts of food or money.

The main Christmas decoration in the home has always been a nativity scene. In December, whole streets are lined with market stalls selling polystyrene grottoes and plaster figures to place in them. In recent years, more and more homes also include a Christmas tree and Santa Claus decorations.

On Christmas Eve some families attend midnight Mass, and then relatives go back to one house together. When they arrive, in the early hours of Christmas day, they have the main Christmas meal of *picana* (pee-CAH-nah). This is a stew with chicken, beef, pork, various vegetables, including chunks of corn and potatoes, and wine or beer. Dessert is custard flan or *pandulce* (pahn-DOOL-say), a bread with nuts and raisins. After the meal family members exchange presents. At two or three in the morning they go to bed.

HISTORIC AND POLITICAL HOLIDAYS

Bolivia also has several holidays that celebrate important historic and political anniversaries. Labor Day is on May 1. Most people who work in labor and activist organizations gather for meetings and speeches, and organized marches are launched. This is in fact a holiday celebrated around the world as a day of protest.

Discovery of America Day is on October 12. This used to be a holiday in Bolivia, but the five hundredth anniversary celebration became a controversial issue in Bolivia. Indigenous Bolivians protested that their ancestors had been in America for hundreds of years before Columbus arrived. The government thus abandoned the holiday.

INTERNET LINKS

www.bolivianlife.com/top-10-festivals-in-bolivia
This article has links to in-depth information about each festival.

www.explorebolivia.com/our-country/festival-calendar
This travel site offers a calendar of festivals in Bolivia.

FOOD

Packages of nuts, quinoa, soya, and lima beans are for sale at a local market.

13

Bolivians often serve a main dish with sides of white rice and white boiled potato, along with *chuño phuti*, a dish made of freeze-dried potatoes, eggs, and cheese.

THERE IS NO TYPICAL BOLIVIAN cuisine. From one region to the next, there is considerable variety. Potatoes are the staple food in the highlands, but in the lowlands they are largely replaced by rice, plantain, and yucca. A family in the Altiplano generally has less access to vegetables and fruit than a family living in the lowlands. Spanish cuisine mixes with indigenous ingredients and Aymara traditions in many areas, while other immigrant groups have also left their marks on the nation's foods. In most Bolivian homes, meats and starches tend to dominate the table.

Bread also plays a large part in the Bolivian diet. Bolivia grows wheat around Santa Cruz and also receives grain from the United States. There are bread sellers on every street corner, and the price is subsidized by the government. The style and taste of bread varies from city to city, but in La Paz, *marraquetas* (marr-ah-KEH-tahs), which look like miniature French loaves, are the most popular.

Llama meat is seldom eaten by middle-class people, who consider it inferior to eat beef. However, llama meat is lower in fat and might well be healthier to consume than beef.

POTATOES AND OTHER TUBERS

Potatoes and other tuberous plants make up a major part of the Bolivian diet. Potatoes come in various sizes and colors, with claims of two or three hundred different varieties being grown in different regions.

Potatoes originated in the Americas and were being eaten by the indigenous people there long before the Spanish arrived. The early conquistadores took potatoes back to Spain and from there their popularity spread throughout northern Europe and the British Isles.

In addition to potatoes, people eat a large number of other kinds of tuberous plants, including *oca* and *anu*. *Oca* is a fleshy root that grows between 2 to 4 inches (5 to 10 cm) long. It looks like a pink sausage and can be boiled, roasted, or fried. Anu is a yellow-white plant that looks and tastes similar to a parsnip. Two other basic foods that are widely eaten are *choclo* (CHOH-kloh), which is a large type of corn, and *habas* beans. Habas beans are collected from the wild and are either roasted or put in stews.

Corn and various types of potatoes are important parts of the Bolivian diet.

THE MEAL PATTERN

A woman enjoys a cup of hot coca tea, or maté, in the Andes.

Breakfast is called *desayuno* (day-sie-OO-noh) and is quite simple, frequently little more than a roll with coffee. Children usually eat bread and either jelly and butter, or cheese, and drink milk with cocoa or drops of coffee. People rushing to work might stop to buy a bowl of chicken soup from a street vendor.

In cities, lunch, or *almuerzo* (al-MWER-zoh), is the most important meal of the day. Many restaurants offer a set lunch, including an appetizer, soup, a beef or chicken dish, and dessert. These are very popular and cost as little as 80 cents. Lunch is a leisurely occasion, even on workdays, and it is not unusual to see businessmen linger over coffee in no apparent rush to get back to work.

On weekends, lunch with family and friends becomes a major social event and can last for a while. At the end of the meal, coffee, tea, or *maté* (MAH-tay), a drink made of plant and flower extractions, is served at the table. Then people move to the garden and resume their conversations. This is known as *sobremesa* (soh-bray-MAY-sah), or the after-lunch hour. Frequently a guest invited for lunch is still there when the evening meal is served.

In rural areas the meal pattern is very different. Altiplano farmers have only two meals a day; the first eaten early in the morning, and the second in the evening after work. The diet in these communities is monotonous, with the basic meal made up of quinoa, oca, and potatoes. Indigenous families usually eat outside if it is not raining. The men, particularly, do not feel comfortable eating openly in front of strangers, so when they are away from home, they usually face a wall when they are eating and sit hunched over their food.

Silpancho is a traditional and filling Bolivian meal of beef, egg, white rice, and potatoes

FAVORITE RECIPES

Most Bolivian recipes have meat in them, and beef, chicken, and fish are popular with people who can afford them. Poorer people generally have to be content with lamb, goat, or llama meat.

One of the most common dinners is *silpancho* (seel-PAN-choh), which is pounded beef with an egg cooked on top. Soups, stews, and broth are very popular in Bolivia. Lamb is often served this way in meals such as *thimpu* (TEEM-poo), which is a spicy stew cooked with vegetables. *Saice* (SIE-say) is another meaty broth, and *fricasé* is a pork stew seasoned with yellow *ají* (a-HEE), or hot pepper.

Hot, spicy sauces are popular additions to any dish. These might be made from tomatoes or pepper pods and are usually placed on the table in a small dish so that people can add as much or as little as they wish.

The lowlands diet includes the meat of many wild animals, particularly armadillo, which are commonly found in the woodlands.

CHUÑO OR FREEZE-DRIED POTATOES

Indigenous groups living on the Altiplano have their own way of freeze-drying potatoes and oca *so that they turn into* chuño *(CHOO-nyoh). Any surplus crop is spread on the ground to freeze at night and then allowed to thaw in the sunlight.*

For several days in a row the vegetables are trampled with bare feet to squeeze out the moisture. This finally leaves a light, dry husk that can be stored for months.

Chuño can be added to stews and soups, and travelers take it on journeys because it rehydrates and cooks quickly.

FRUITS AND DESSERTS

Bolivia has an excellent selection of fruits. These include several fruits that are not easily found in the United States: custard apples, prickly pear cactus, passion fruit, and a range of mangos.

Desserts with a local flavor include *tojori* (toh-HOH-ree) and *thaya* (TIE-ah). With the consistency of porridge, tojori is made from corn, cinnamon, and sugar all mashed together. Thaya are a favorite on the Altiplano and are made from apple puree mixed with sugared water and spiced with cinnamon and cloves. This mixture is shaped into little domes and placed on the roofs of houses to freeze overnight. In the morning a little sugar water colored with local spices is added. The town of Potosí specializes in pastries, including *tawa-tawas*, which are deep-fried pastries served in syrup.

A special dessert saved for festivals are *confites* (kohn-FEE-tays), which are made by local confectioners and sold on festival days. They are made from boiled sugar syrup hardened around nuts, aniseed, fruit, biscuits, or coconuts, and they come in an amazing variety of colors.

In rural areas, guinea pigs often have free run of the house, surviving on scraps that fall to the floor, but at fiesta time they become a favorite delicacy.

Saltenas are a favorite meat-filled Bolivian pastry that is commonly sold on the street.

STREET FOOD

In the cities, the favorite snack is the *salteña* (sal-TAY-nyah). These little oval pies are eaten as a quick lunch or a tasty and filling snack. Salteñas are stuffed with chicken or beef and whatever else is available. This might include different vegetables, such as potatoes and onions, and eggs. The final touch is a big helping of spices to give the pies their distinctive taste. Salteñas are the subject of considerable debate, and everyone seems to know one shop or stall that bakes the very best in town.

Empanadas (em-pah-NAH-dahs) are filled with either beef, chicken, or cheese. They can be baked in bread or deep-fried in fat. Another fast food specialty is *humintas* (oo-MEEN-tahs). These are made from cornmeal with various additional fillings, shaped into a triangle, and wrapped in a corn husk. Like salteñas, they come in many different varieties.

Bolivia's traditional fast foods are coming under considerable competition from burgers and fries. In the big cities these are sold from little kiosks on almost every street and are extremely popular.

DRINKS

Black tea is probably the most common Bolivian drink. It is served strong, with lots of sugar. *Maté de coca* (MAH-tay day KOH-kah), which is tea with coca leaves added, is also very popular and is said to be a good cure for altitude sickness.

Refresco (ray-FRES-koh) is a fruit juice. *Tostada* (tohs-TA-da) is made from a combination of barley, honey, cinnamon, cloves, and water. These are mixed in plastic containers and poured into glasses lined up for thirsty customers. A metal saucer is placed on top to keep the dirt and dust out.

Chicha is a potent, homemade corn beer that has been brewed since Incan times and probably for hundreds of years before then. To make chicha, women chew corn into small balls called *muko* (MOO-koh) and leave them to dry in the sun. The muko are then boiled with chunks of meat, grain, and sugar. Spices give a regional flavor to each brew. Local people know which houses chicha is brewed in, and on festival days people walk around the streets selling it by the glass.

There is also a drink called *singani* (seen-GAH-nee) that is made from grapes and is a cross between whiskey and wine.

A freshly made juice is made with local fruit, such as this banana passionfruit juice.

INTERNET LINKS

www.bolivianlife.com/a-guide-to-bolivias-best-foods

This travel site gives an overview of some of Bolivia's best known dishes.

www.boliviaweb.com/recipes/english

This site offers some authentic Bolivian recipes in English using mostly easily available ingredients.

www.travelandleisure.com/articles/dig-in-street-food-in-la-paz-bolivia

This article takes a quick tour of street snacks in La Paz.

PICANTE DE POLLO (SPICY CHICKEN)

4- or 5-pound (1,350 grams) chicken, cut into eight parts
¼ cup (60 milliliters) oil
¼ cup (60 mL) powdered chili pepper
2 cups (300 grams) white onion, finely chopped
1 small can diced tomato
½ cup (75 g) fresh serrano pepper (or other medium-hot pepper), finely chopped
1 cup (150 g) green peas
1 teaspoon ground cumin
1 teaspoon crumbled oregano
½ teaspoon ground black pepper
1 teaspoon salt
3 garlic cloves, chopped
3 cups (700 mL) chicken broth or water
½ cup (75 g) parsley, chopped

In a large Dutch oven or heavy covered pot, brown the chicken pieces in the oil. Add the remaining ingredients, except the peas, and cover with the broth or water.

Bring to a boil, then lower heat and cover. Simmer for about 45 minutes, or until the chicken is soft. Stir occasionally. Add more liquid if needed. Add peas and cook 5 more minutes. Serve in a deep plate, with long-grained white rice, a peeled, boiled white potato, and a small salad. Sprinkle all with chopped parsley.

TAWA TAWAS (BOLIVIAN FRIED BREAD)

2 cups (220 grams) flour
2 tsp baking powder
3 tsp granulated sugar
1 tsp salt
1 Tbsp (15 g) butter, melted
2 eggs
¼ cup (60 milliliters) milk
¼ cup water (60 mL), room-temperature
Canola or other frying oil
Sugar cane syrup, honey, or powdered sugar

In a large bowl, whisk together flour, baking powder and salt.

In another bowl, lightly beat the eggs. Add the butter, milk and water, and mix well.

Add the egg mixture to the flour mixture, and mix well until it forms a dough.

Turn the dough onto a floured surface and knead until the dough is smooth, about 2 minutes.

Cover dough with a clean kitchen towel and allow it to rest for 10 to 15 minutes.

Working with one half or one third of the dough at a time, roll it out on a floured surface until it is about one-eighth inch thick.

Using a sharp knife or a pizza wheel, cut the dough into rectangles about 1½ inches by 4 inches long. Cover and allow dough pieces to rest about 5 minutes.

Meanwhile, place oil in a deep fryer, or fill oil no more than half-way up the side of a heavy skillet. Heat to about 375-degrees Fahrenheit (190 °C).

Fry five or six pieces of dough at a time, turning to cook both sides, until puffed and golden. Drain fried pastries on paper towels.

Brush or drizzle with sugar cane syrup or honey. Sprinkle with powdered sugar.

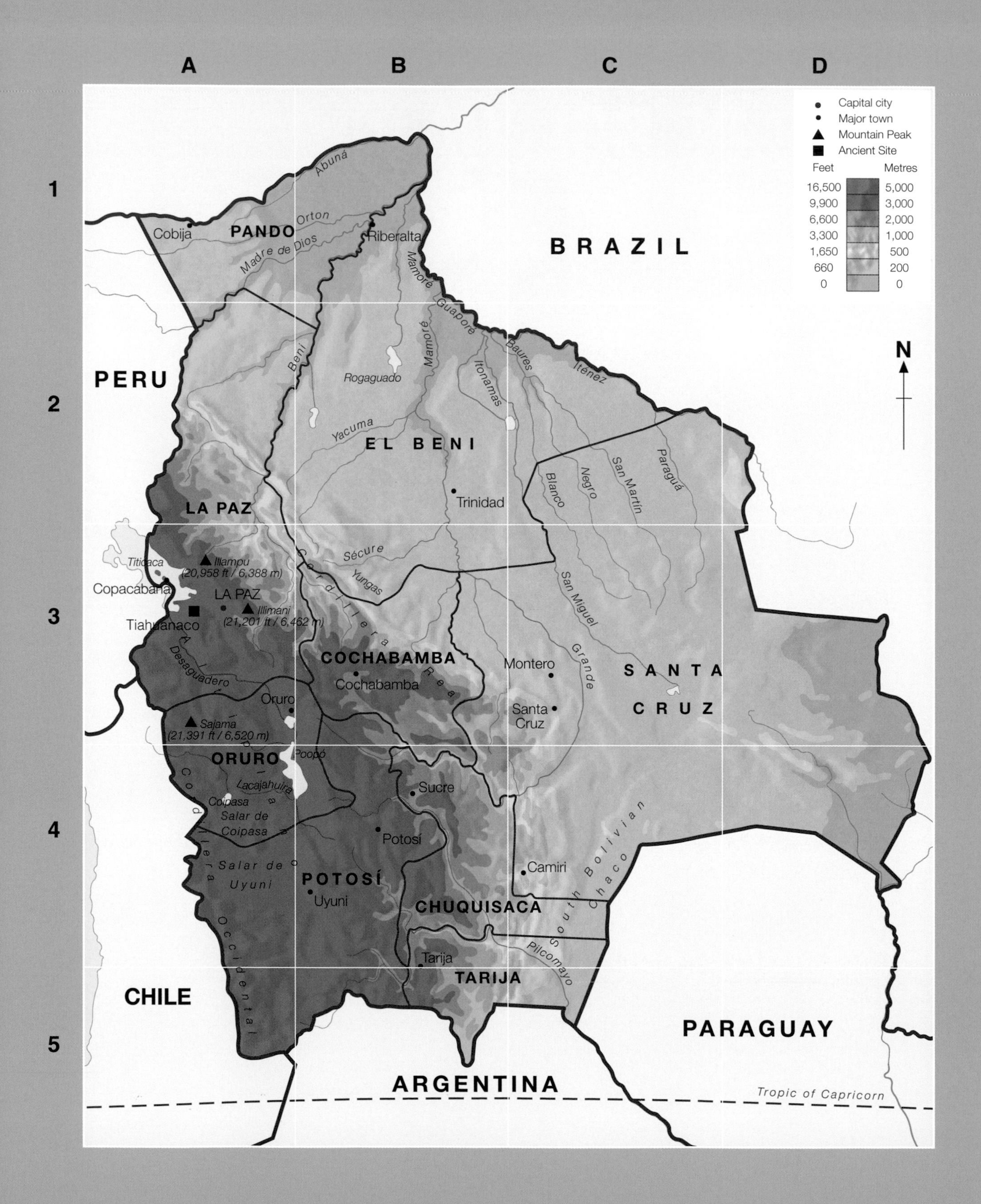

A
B
C
D
1
2
3
4
5
Capital city
Major town
Mountain Peak
Ancient Site
Feet
Metres
16,500
5,000
9,900
3,000
6,600
2,000
3,300
1,000
1,650
500
660
200
0
0
N
BRAZIL
PERU
CHILE
PARAGUAY
ARGENTINA
Tropic of Capricorn
PANDO
Cobija
Abuná
Orton
Madre de Dios
Riberalta
Mamoré
Guaporé
Beni
Rogaguado
Itonamas
Baures
Iténez
Yacuma
EL BENI
Trinidad
Blanco
Negro
San Martín
Paraguá
LA PAZ
Titicaca
Illampu
(20,958 ft / 6,388 m)
Copacabana
LA PAZ
Illimani
(21,201 ft / 6,462 m)
Tiahuanaco
Sécure
Yungas
Cordillera Real
San Miguel
Grande
Desaguadero
COCHABAMBA
Cochabamba
Montero
SANTA CRUZ
Santa Cruz
Oruro
Sajama
(21,391 ft / 6,520 m)
ORURO
Poopó
Lacajahuira
Coipasa
Salar de Coipasa
Salar de Uyuni
Cordillera Occidental
Sucre
Potosí
POTOSÍ
Uyuni
Camiri
South Bolivian Chaco
CHUQUISACA
Pilcomayo
Tarija
TARIJA

MAP OF BOLIVIA

Abuná River, B1
Argentina, B5

Baures River, C2
Beni River, B2
Blanco River, C2
Brazil, C1

Camiri, C4
Chile, A5
Chuquisaca, B4
Cobija, A1
Cochabamba Province, B3
Cochabamba Town, B3
Coipasa Lake, A4
Coipasa, Salar de, A4
Copacabana, A3
Cordillera Occidental, A4
Cordillera Real, B3

Desaguadero River, A3

El Beni, B2

Grande River, C3
Guaporé River, B2

Illampu, Mount, A3
Illimani, Mount, A3
Itenez River, C2
Itonamas River, B2

La Paz Capital, A3
La Paz Province, A2
Lacajahuira River, B4

Madre de Dios River, A1
Mamoré River, B2
Montero, C3

Negro River, C2

Orton River, B1
Oruro Province, A4
Oruro Town, A3

Pando, A1
Paraguá River, C2
Paraguay, C5
Peru, A2
Pilcomayo River, C4
Poopó, Lake, B4
Potosí Province, B4
Potosí Town, B4

Riberalta, B1
Rogaguado Lake, B2

Sajama, Mount, A3
San Martín River, C2
San Miguel River, C3
Santa Cruz Province, C3
Santa Cruz Town, C3
Sécure River, B3
South Bolivian Chaco, C4
Sucre, B4

Tarija Province, B5
Tarija Town, B4
Tiahuanaco, A3
Titicaca, Lake, A3
Trinidad, B2
Tropic of Capricorn, D5

Uyuni, B4
Uyuni, Salar de, A4

Yacuma River, B2
Yungas, B3

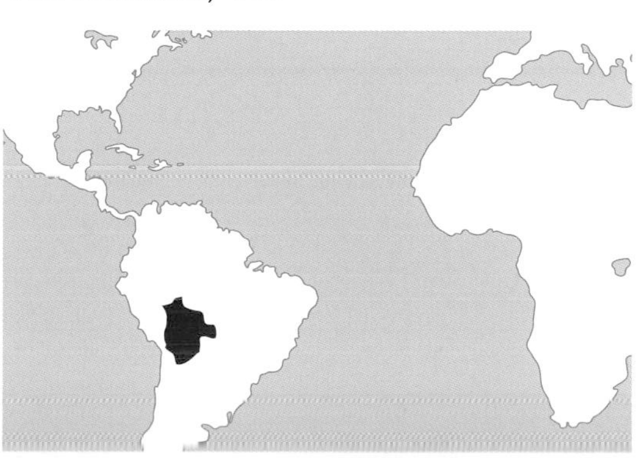

ECONOMIC BOLIVIA

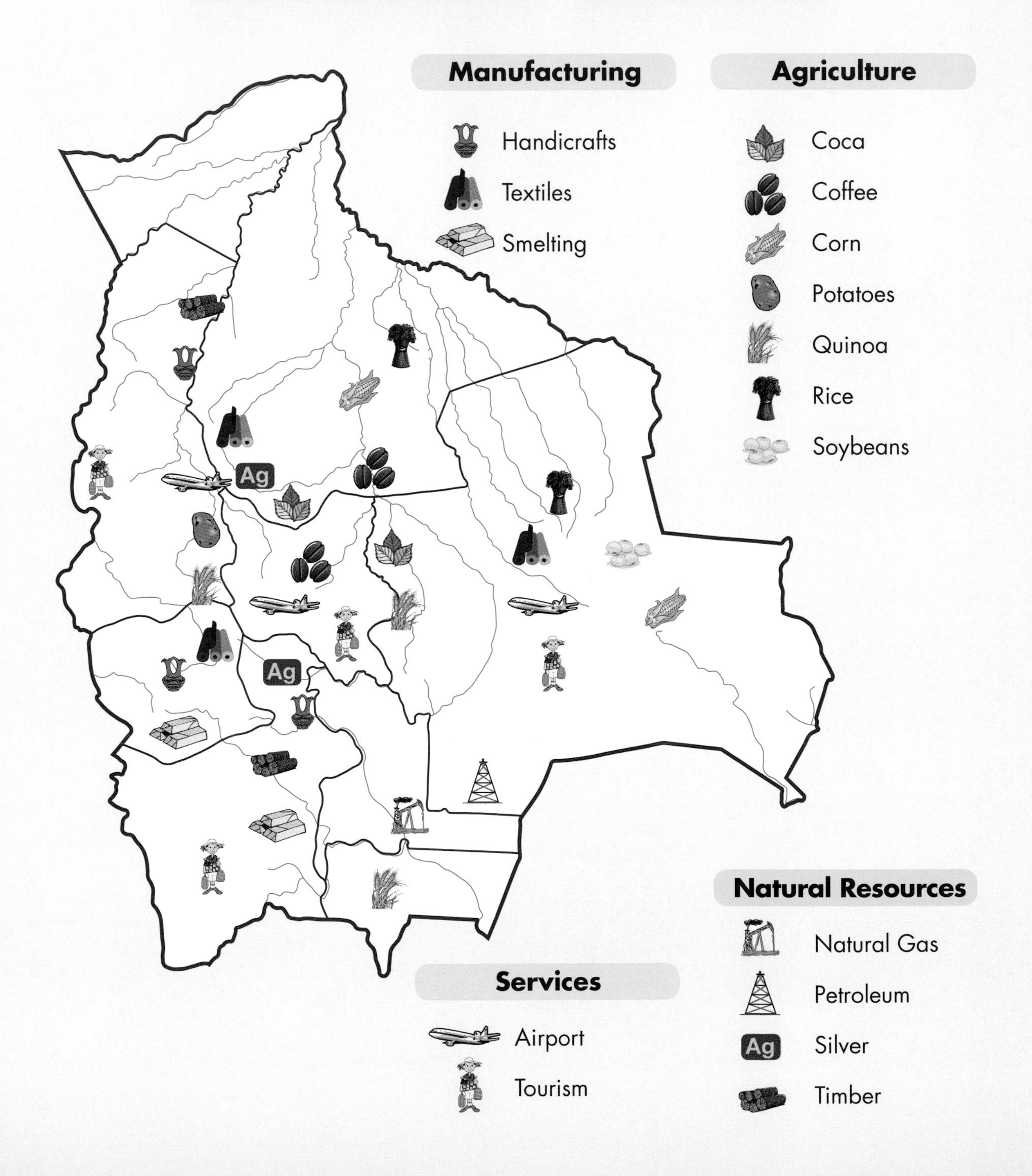

ABOUT THE ECONOMY

GROSS DOMESTIC PRODUCT (GDP)
$33.24 billion (2014)

GDP PER CAPITA
$6,200 (2014)

GDP BY SECTOR
Agriculture, 13.2 percent; industry, 38.7 percent; services, 48 percent (2014)

WORKFORCE
4.88 million (2014)

UNEMPLOYMENT RATE
7.3 percent (in urban areas); but widespread underemployment (2014)

POPULATION BELOW POVERTY LINE
45 percent (2011)

INFLATION RATE
5.8 percent (2014)

CURRENCY
1 boliviano (BOB) = 100 cents
Notes: 2, 5, 10, 20, 50, 100, 200 BOB
Coins: 1 BOB; 2, 5, 10, 20, 50 cents
USD 1 = 6.91 bolivianos (January 2016)

AGRICULTURE PRODUCTS
Soybeans, quinoa, Brazil nuts, sugarcane, coffee, corn, rice, potatoes, chia, coca.

INDUSTRIAL PRODUCTS
Mining, smelting, petroleum, food and beverages, tobacco, handicrafts, clothing, jewelry

EXPORT PARTNERS
Brazil, Argentina, United States, Colombia, Peru (2014)

IMPORT PARTNERS
China, Brazil, United States, Argentina, Peru, Japan, Chile (2014)

CULTURAL BOLIVIA

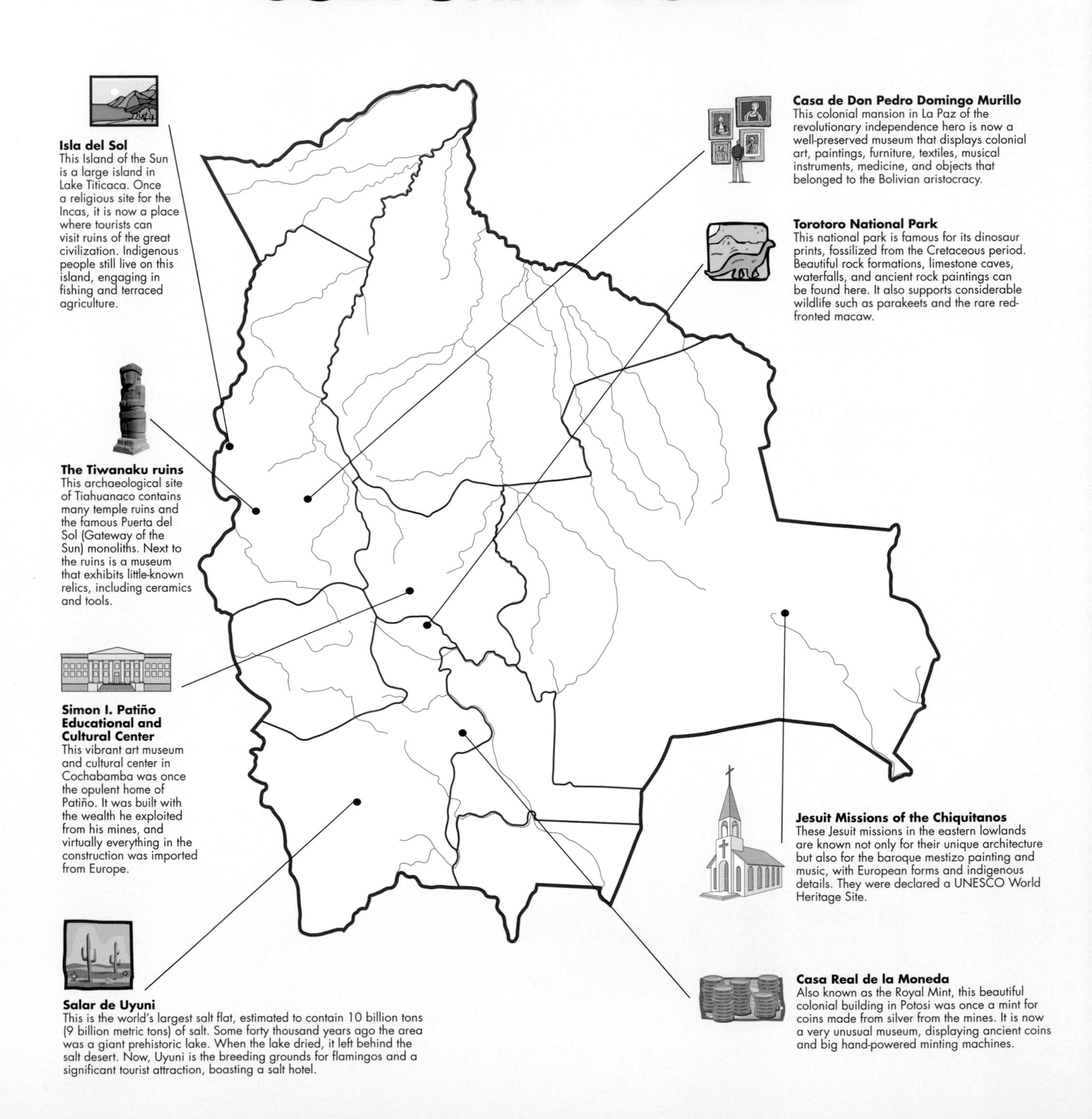

ABOUT THE CULTURE

OFFICIAL NAME
Plurinational State of Bolivia

AREA
424,165 square miles (1,098,581 sq km)

CAPITAL
La Paz (seat of government); Sucre (legal capital and seat of judiciary)

DEPARTMENTS
Chuquisaca, Cochabamba, Beni, La Paz, Oruro, Pando, Potosí, Santa Cruz, Tarija

MAJOR LAKES
Lake Titicaca, Lake Poopó

MAJOR RIVERS
Beni, Mamoré, Desaguadero, Pilcomayo, Paraguay

HIGHEST POINT
Mount Sajama 21,391 feet (6,519 m)

POPULATION
10,800,882 (2015)

LIFE EXPECTANCY
Approximately 69 years;
Men 66 years, women 72 years (2015)

ETHNIC GROUPS
mestizo (mixed white and Amerindian ancestry), 68 percent; indigenous, 20 percent; white, 5 percent; cholo/chola, 2 percent; black, 1 percent; other, 1 percent; unspecified, 3 percent; (44 percent of respondents indicated feeling part of some indigenous group, predominantly Quechua or Aymara) (2009)

OFFICIAL LANGUAGES
Spanish (60.7 percent), Quechua (21.2 percent), Aymara (14.6 percent)
Note: Bolivia's 2009 constitution designates Spanish and all indigenous languages as official; thirty-six indigenous languages are specified, including some that are extinct.

PRESIDENT
Evo Morales (2005–)

LITERACY RATE
Approximately 87.4 percent;
Men 93.1 percent, women 81.6 percent

RELIGIONS
Roman Catholic, 76.8 percent; Evangelical and Pentecostal, 8.1 percent; Protestant, 7.9 percent; other, 1.7 percent; none, 5.5 percent (2012)

TIMELINE

IN BOLIVIA	IN THE WORLD
500–800 CE Tiwanaku civilization emerged.	**600 CE** Height of Mayan civilization
	1000 The Chinese perfect gunpowder and begin to use it in warfare.
1476–1532 Height of the Incan civilization.	**1530** Beginning of transatlantic slave trade organized by the Portuguese in Africa.
1538 The Spanish conquer Bolivia. Beginning of three centuries of colonial rule.	
1544 Silver is discovered in Potosí.	**1558–1603** Reign of Elizabeth I of England
	1620 Pilgrims sail the *Mayflower* to America.
	1776 US Declaration of Independence
1781 Tupac Katari and Bartolina Sisa lead indigenous rebellion.	**1789–1799** The French Revolution
1825 Bolivia becomes independent, with Simon Bolivar as president.	**1861** The US Civil War begins.
1879–1883 Pacific War with Chile. Bolivia loses its coast to Chile.	
1899–1903 Arce War with Brazil. Bolivia loses more territories.	**1914** World War I begins.
1932–1935 Chaco War with Paraguay.	**1939–1945** World War II.
1952 Revolution by peasants and miners. The MNR, led by Víctor Paz Estenssoro, takes power.	**1957** The Russians launch *Sputnik 1*.
1964 Military coup by René Barrietos.	

IN BOLIVIA	IN THE WORLD
1967 Che Guevara is assassinated in Bolivia.	**1966–1969** The Chinese Cultural Revolution.
1971 Military coups.	
1982 Democracy is reestablished.	
1985 Paz Estenssoro becomes president again and enacts economic reforms.	**1986** Nuclear power disaster at Chernobyl in Ukraine
1989 Jaime Paz Zamora becomes president in coalition with longtime enemy Hugo Bánzer Suárez.	**1991** Breakup of the Soviet Union
1993 Gonzálo Sánchez de Lozada becomes president.	
1997 Former dictator Hugo Bánzer Suárez elected president.	**1997** Hong Kong is returned to China.
2000 Water War breaks out. Social conflict in Bolivia.	**2001** Terrorists crash planes in New York, Washington, DC, and Pennsylvania.
2002 Gonzálo Sánchez is elected president again.	
2003 Gas War; Sánchez is forced to resign.	**2003** War in Iraq starts.
2005 Evo Morales wins election, becoming the first indigenous president in Bolivian history.	
2006 Morales nationalizes most of Bolivia's natural gas fields.	**2008** United States elects its first African American president, Barack Obama.
2009 Morales enacts new constitution, giving indigenous people more rights.	
2015 Pope Francis visits Bolivia.	**2015** Islamist terrorists attack Paris.

GLOSSARY

Altiplano (ahl-tee-PLAH-noh)
Also known as the High Plateau, a large expanse of high, flat land between two ranges of the Andes.

amauta **(ah-MOW-tah)**
Wise men who traditonally memorized vast amounts of information.

bombín **(bohm-BEEN)**
Bolivian name for a bowler hat, frequently worn by indigenous highland women.

cha'lla **(CHAH-ya)**
A ritual blessing, frequently drawn from a combination of Christian and indigenous beliefs.

chulla **(CHOO-lah)**
A woolen knit hat with ear flaps worn by indigenous men.

chuño **(CHOO-nyoh)**
Potatoes that have been frozen and then dried in the sun.

cucho **(KOO-choh)**
A ritual offering placed in the foundation of a new building.

manta **(MAHN-Tah)**
Shawl worn by indigenous highland women that can be folded to carry babies or other loads.

padrino **(pah-DREE-noh)**
Godparent.

quenas **(KAY-nas)**
Flutes made from reed pipes.

salteñas **(sal-TAY-nyahs)**
Spicy meat pies often eaten as a snack.

sobremesa **(soh-bray-MAY-sah)**
The after-lunch hour, when people talk.

surazo **(soo-RAH-zoh)**
Cold winds that blow in from the Argentine pampas.

viernes de soltero **(VYAIR-nays day sol-TAY-roh)**
Literally "single on Friday," the Hispanic custom for men to go out without their wives on Friday nights to drink and play dice.

FOR FURTHER INFORMATION

BOOKS

Farthing, Linda C. and Benjamin H. Kohl. Evo's Bolivia: Continuity and Change. Austin, TX: University of Texas Press, 2014.

Lonely Planet, Greg Benchwick, and Paul Smith. Lonely Planet Bolivia. Oakland, CA: Lonely Planet, 2013.

Sánchez-H., José. My Mother's Bolivian Kitchen. New York: Hippocrene Books, Inc., 2005.

Werner, Robert J. Bolivia in Focus: A Guide to the People, Politics, and Culture. Northampton, MA.: Interlink Publishing Group, Inc., 2009.

DVDS/FILMS

Che 2. Directed by Steven Soderbergh. IFC Films, 2008.

Cocalero. Directed by Alejandro Landes. First Run Features, 2007.

Cuestión de Fe. Directed by Marcos Loayza. Iconoscopio, 1995.

Even the Rain. Directed by Iciar Bollian. Lionsgate, 2011.

La Sangre del Cóndor. Directed by Jorge Sanginés. Grupo Ukamau, 1969.

Our Brand Is Crisis. Directed by Rachel Boynton. Koch Lorber Films, 2006.

The Devil's Miner. Directed by Kief Davidson and Richard Ladkani. First Run Features, 2006.

MUSIC

30 Años Solo Vive Una Vez. Los Kjarkas. Mambo Maniacs, 2003. (Bolivian folk music)

Nunca más! Atajo. Pro Audio, 2003. (Rock, blues, and folk fusion)

Soy De Sangre, Quechua Y Aymara. Fortaleza. Flying Fish, 2015. (Bolivian folk music)

WEBSITES

BBC News. Bolivia Country Profile. news.bbc.co.uk/2/hi/americas/country_profiles/1210487.stm

Bolivia, Plurinational State of. Embassy in Washington, DC. www.bolivia-usa.org

CIA World Factbook. *Bolivia*. www.cia.gov/library/publications/the-world-factbook/geos/bl.html

National Geographic, "Bolivia's Brink." http://ngm.nationalgeographic.com/2008/07/bolivias-new-order/alma-guillermoprieto-text

US Department of State. US Relations With Bolivia. www.state.gov/r/pa/ei/bgn/35751.htm

BIBLIOGRAPHY

Achtenberg, Emily. "From Water Wars to Water Scarcity: Bolivia's Cautionary Tale." NACLA, June 5, 2013. https://nacla.org/blog/2013/6/5/water-wars-water-scarcity-bolivia%E2%80%99s-cautionary-tale.

BBC News. "Profile: Bolivia's President Evo Morales." October 13, 2014. http://www.bbc.com/news/world-latin-america-12166905.

Blais, Andre and Louis Massicote. *Establishing the Rules of the Game: Election Laws in Democracies*. Toronto: University of Toronto Press, 2003.

Guillermoprieto, Alma, "Bolivia's New Order." *National Geographic*, July 2008. http://ngm.nationalgeographic.com/2008/07/bolivias-new-order/alma-guillermoprieto-text.

Gustafson, Bret. "Language Rights And Guarani Renaissance In Bolivia." Carnegie Council for Ethics in International Affairs, April 22, 2005. http://www.carnegiecouncil.org/en_US/publications/archive/dialogue/2_12/section_1/5141.html.

The Holy See. "Address of the Holy Father at the Second World Meeting of Popular Movements" (transcript), Santa Cruz, Bolivia, July 9, 2015. w2.vatican.va/content/francesco/en/speeches/2015/july/documents/papa-francesco_20150709_bolivia-movimenti-popolari.html.

Kozak, Robert. "Bolivia Cuts Coca Production for Fourth Consecutive Year, U.N. Says." *Wall Street Journal*, August 17, 2015. http://www.wsj.com/articles/bolivia-cuts-coca-production-for-fourth-consecutive-year-u-n-says-1439835780.

New Agriculturist. Country Profile: Bolivia. http://www.new-ag.info/en/country/profile.php?a=3155.

Requejo, Ferran, and Miquel Caminal. *Political Liberalism and Plurinational Democracies*. New York: Routledge, Taylor & Francis Group, 2010.

Rigby, Rhymer. "Bolivia: A spell in a high place." *The Telegraph Travel*, February 9, 2004. http://www.telegraph.co.uk/travel/destinations/southamerica/bolivia/729642/Bolivia-A-spell-in-a-high-place.html.

US Department of State. Bolivia: International Religious Freedom Report 2007 http://www.state.gov/j/drl/rls/irf/2007/90243.htm.

———. US Relations With Bolivia. http://www.state.gov/r/pa/ei/bgn/35751.htm.

Yardley, Jim and William Neuman. "In Bolivia, Pope Francis Apologizes for Church's 'Grave Sins'." *New York Times*, July 9, 2015. http://www.nytimes.com/2015/07/10/world/americas/pope-francis-bolivia-catholic-church-apology.html.

INDEX

African, 25, 63, 67, 69–70, 99, 139
Altiplano, 12, 14–16, 18–19, 21, 23, 49–50, 64, 66, 68–69, 73, 76, 81–82, 102, 112, 123, 125, 127
altitude sickness, 75, 76, 110
Amazon, 5, 12, 14, 56–58, 61
Andes, 6, 12–15, 18, 25, 28, 42, 50, 56, 61, 63, 72, 82, 104, 112–113, 119, 125
animals, 18, 24, 56–57, 65, 73, 77, 86–87, 89, 97, 102, 120, 126
Aymara, 6, 22, 35, 64–67, 69, 71, 80–81, 83, 87, 93–96, 101, 103–104, 116, 120, 137

Bánzer, Hugo, 32–33, 139
Bolívar, Simón, 27–28, 111
bombín, 83
bowler, 69, 83, 100–101
boys, 7, 46, 48, 74, 77, 79, 81, 102, 108–109
Brazil, 11–12, 49, 51, 133, 135, 138

Cassidy, Butch, 103, 105
Castro, Fidel, 34
Catavi tin mine, 31
Catholic / Catholicism, 5, 7, 38, 67, 85, 88–90, 119, 137, 139
Chaco War, 29–30, 138
Chagas disease, 76
cha'lla, 89, 91
Chávez, Hugo, 8
child labor, 46, 48, 51, 53
children, 51, 53, 65, 71, 74, 77, 79–80, 91–92, 100, 108, 110–111, 120, 125
Chile, 6, 12–13, 29, 42–43, 49, 95, 133, 135, 138
Christmas, 107, 118, 120–121
Chúngara, Domitila, 82
chuño, 123, 127
CIA (US Central Intelligence Agency), 31
coca, 6, 9, 25, 32, 34–35, 39, 48, 52–53, 60, 75, 87, 89, 91, 120, 125, 128, 135
cocaine, 9, 25, 34, 52, 75
Cochabamba, 12, 32–33, 47, 51–52, 56, 64, 70, 99, 110, 133, 137
colonial era, 5, 19, 27, 90, 96, 99, 101, 138–139
constitution, 6, 9, 34–35, 37–39, 42–43, 47, 55, 63, 85, 93–94, 137, 139
Copacabana, 17, 88, 114–115, 133
Creole, 26
cucho, 89

dance, 5, 22, 99, 101–102, 108–109, 113, 115, 118
deforestation, 57–58, 61
dictator, 32, 139

Ekeko, 87, 116
Estenssoro, Víctor Paz, 30, 32, 139
folklore, 19, 25, 86, 103, 117, 119

girls, 78–79, 81
gold, 17, 19, 22, 24, 42, 47–48, 60, 101
Gran Chaco, 12, 29
Gran Poder, 118–119
Guarachi, Bernardo, 112, 113
Guevara, Che, 31, 139

health, 25, 50, 60, 66, 74, 75, 76, 78, 111

Illimani, Mount, 13–14, 102, 112, 133
Inca, 5, 19, 22, 24–26, 50, 56, 66, 73, 86–87, 91, 95, 100–101, 115, 119–120, 128, 138
indigenous, 6, 9, 13, 25–26, 30, 32, 34–36, 38, 40–42, 46, 50, 52, 56, 63–64, 66–69, 74–75, 79–81, 85, 87, 89–90, 93–95, 100–102, 105, 108, 120–121, 123–125, 127, 137–139

Japanese, 47, 71, 94

La Paz, 6, 9, 12–14, 17–19, 23, 25–26, 30, 36–37, 41–43, 47, 49, 51, 56, 59, 64, 69–70, 76–77, 80, 83, 89, 91, 94, 98, 102, 107, 109–112, 116, 118–119, 123, 129, 133, 137–138

INDEX

lithium, 5, 47
llamas, 16, 18, 91, 96–97, 100, 120, 124, 126

manta, 81
mestizo, 42, 63, 69, 80, 85, 87, 102, 137
minerals, 5, 14, 42, 47, 60
miners, 25, 31, 47–48, 52, 60, 82, 118–119, 139
mines / mining, 25–26, 29, 30, 33, 47–48, 51, 53, 55, 60, 69, 74, 82, 103, 117, 119, 135
Morales, Evo, 6–9, 12, 34–35, 39, 41, 43, 45, 52, 61, 75, 82, 90, 93, 137, 139
mountains, 5, 13–15, 17, 21, 25, 33, 54–55, 88, 112–113
Movement for Socialism (MAS), 34, 39–41

natural gas, 6, 12, 32, 39, 49, 139

oil, 12, 29–30, 33, 47, 49, 51, 56, 130–131, 138
Oruro, 15, 25, 101, 117–118, 133, 137

Pachamama, 55, 86–87, 89, 91, 119
padrino, 77
Paraguay, 11–12, 15, 29, 87, 90, 106, 133, 137–138
Peru, 12, 17, 19, 22, 25–29, 42–43, 51, 65, 70, 75, 95, 102, 119, 133, 135
picante de pollo (recipe), 130
plurinational, 7, 37–38, 40–41, 63
pollution, 59–60
Poopó, Lake 15, 18, 133, 137
Pope Francis, 7, 89–90, 139
Potosi, 25, 99
poverty, 8–9, 34, 45, 53, 58, 59, 71, 77, 82, 135

Quechua, 22, 64–65, 80–81, 87–88, 94–97, 137
quenas, 104
quinoa, 44–45, 50, 53, 65–66, 122, 125, 135

revolution, 26–28, 30, 33, 38, 49, 64, 69, 74, 138–139
rivers, 12, 14–15, 57, 59–60, 68, 133

salt flat, 5, 15, 66
salteña, 128
Santa Cruz, 7–8, 19, 49, 51, 71, 90, 94, 111, 123, 133, 137
sea, 6, 11, 13–14, 25, 29, 43, 46, 86
silver, 14, 17, 22, 24–26, 29, 47–48, 55, 88, 101, 111, 117, 138
sobremesa, 125
soccer, 7, 70, 106–111, 113
Spain, 24–26, 28, 68, 93, 96–97, 124
Spanish, 5, 7, 17, 22, 24–28, 50, 63, 66, 68–69, 79, 85–88, 92–97, 99, 101–102, 104, 115–116, 123–124, 137–138
Sucre, 11–12, 18–19, 26–28, 37, 40, 51, 64, 84–85, 102, 105, 133, 137
surazo, 15

tawa tawas, 127, 131(recipe)
Titicaca, Lake, 14–19, 21–23, 60, 64–66, 73, 86, 101, 109, 115–116, 133, 137
Tiwanaku, 20–22, 66, 86
tourists, 5, 101, 117

UNESCO, 23, 55, 99, 105, 118
United States, 7–8, 31, 34, 43, 45, 49, 52, 61, 75, 78, 102–103, 120, 123, 127, 135, 138–139
viernes de soltero, 113
Water War, 32–33, 139
weaving, 5, 98–100, 105, 108
wildlife, 18, 55–58
Wiphala, 42
women, 40, 65, 67, 69, 74, 78–83, 100–102, 105, 108, 111, 120, 129, 137

Yungas, 12, 15–16, 49, 52, 56, 69–71, 101, 113, 133

zampoña, 104